FOOTBALL
the golden age

BALL
age

John Tennant

CASSELL&CO

First published in Great Britain in
2001 by Cassell & Co

Copyright © John Tennant 2001

The moral right of John Tennant
to be identified as the author of
this work has been asserted in
accordance with the Copyright,
Designs and Patents Act of 1988.

Cassell & Co acknowledge the
assistance provided by Getty
Images/Hulton Getty.

Hulton|Archive

A CIP catalogue record for
this book is available from the
British Library.

ISBN 0304 359963

Printed and bound in Italy
by Canale

Cassell & Co
Wellington House
125 Strand
London WC2R 0BB

I. **foreword** 6

II. **introduction by Rodney Marsh** 8

III. **the photographs** 10

IV. **index** 380

V. **photographic credits** 383

VI. **acknowledgements** 384

FOREWORD

'Even now, whenever I arrive at any football ground,
or merely pass close to one when it is silent, I experience
a unique alerting of the senses. The moment evokes
my past in an instantaneous emotional rapport which is
more certain, more secret, than memory.'

'THE FOOTBALL MAN' BY ARTHUR HOPCRAFT

PHOTOGRAPHS OF THE 'DECISIVE MOMENTS' in football matches, particularly goals, are a staple of tomorrow's sports pages. Very soon after the points are won these action pictures lose their edge and are dull; their shelf-life is short. And any significance derives from their being proof of an important victory more than any intrinsic photographic merit.

So this collection of photographs is not about 'action'; there are no match-turning tricks or last-minute winners. It is concerned with things more romantic and idiosyncratic than just 'Goals On Camera': the seemingly inconsequential moments that every fan cherishes.

My dad took me to see the 1963 Cup Final. In spite of the excitement of the occasion, all memory of the match, its incidents, near misses, fouls and goals is hazy, distorted and somehow irrelevant. But nearly forty years later I still clearly remember fussing over which particular 'lucky' rosette to buy (I chose well). And the 'Orange Fruitie' I enjoyed on the bus after the game.

So that much of what fascinates me about football is an adjunct to the game itself. The thrill of a match encompasses more than the 90 minutes played out on the pitch: it embraces the sight and sound of the crowd and the journey to and from the ground. I have tried to capture the curiosity that is football — a mix of superstition, celebrity, science, devotion, humour and the plain ridiculous — in the photographs I have selected. Look at the automated ball-throwing machine on page 18 and the 'Tornado' boots on page 129. They may seem comical now but we do not know how kind time will be to the high-tech kit in use today — or to Adidas Predators.

It is not only football that has exploited technological advances. Photography began to take a firm hold in daily newspapers after World War I, and right up to the late Fifties it was usual for photographers covering football matches to shoot on plate cameras, with perhaps a maximum of ten frames for the entire game. Even in this time before the stranglehold of television, portraiture and other background stories were all tackled with the same economy. Today, motor-driven cameras are capable of squeezing off five frames a second.

Wherever possible, the photographs are attributed, although most of the old picture agencies operated on the basis that their names, not those of individual photographers, were credited. In the earliest images the 'unknown photographer' is well represented. Some names may be, deservedly, familiar: Bill Brandt, Bert Hardy, Kurt Hutton and Reg Speller, for example; and, more recently, Terry Fincher, Terry O'Neill, Kent Gavin, Ray Green and Monty Fresco.

Many of the images in this selection have been found in newspaper libraries — the 'Daily Herald', 'Daily Express' and 'Evening Standard' — and the 'Picture Post' archive. As well as at agency collections such as Fox, Keystone and Planet News.

The photographs have been chosen because they are arresting in their own right, not just because a player or club happened to achieve greatness. Some players, brilliant on the field but more reserved off it, may not be included. Others, more outgoing, appear more than once; clearly they enjoyed playing to the crowd and the camera. Similarly, the book looks beyond the polarised focus of the national press: the glamorous, successful sides (or those in difficulties) on one hand and a sideways regard for the 'giant-killing' underdog on the other.

As for the book's title, football may be said to have entered its 'golden age' around the beginning of the twentieth century. In 1905 Middlesborough paid Sunderland £1,000 for inside-forward Alf Common. And throughout the game, increasingly skilful players, combined with growing tactical awareness, were routinely attracting huge crowds.

Between then and now — most significantly — England won the World Cup in 1966, an event that has skewed our perception and expectations of football forever.

But perhaps what separates that burst of interest a hundred years ago – together with the great sides of the Twenties and Thirties and the swashbuckling teams and glamorous stars of the Fifties, Sixties and Seventies to which it gave rise – from the increasingly corporate entertainment we follow today is the common spirit that links the majority of the photographs in this book, which, if push became shove and led to a yellow card, may be defined as 'innocence'.

And if in the Eighties this 'golden age' ended, then it would only be fashionable to blame Big Business: TV, all-seater stadia, astronomical wage bills and the rise and rise of the ubiquitous agent. We have taken our sporting heroes and turned them into celebrities.

The difference between Stanley Matthews and David Beckham? A few million pounds a year and an excess of petulance. Stanley wore longer shorts and didn't marry a Spice Girl. And nobody except Stanley Matthews wore Stanley Matthew's shirt. But they share what matters — the gift: creating expectation every time the ball is at their feet. JOHN TENNANT

INTRODUCTION by Rodney Marsh

I REMEMBER Terry O'Neill's photograph of 'The Clan' vividly [see pages 370–371]. We'd just enjoyed a slap-up lunch at a Fleet Street restaurant; the booze had been flowing and we were only too pleased to pose for Terry, who was a friend of mine and some of the others who were there. Even during the relaxed Seventies, this photograph, capturing as it does some of the cream of the nation's professional footballers, large cigars in hand and looking more like the cast of a Hollywood movie, was something of a coup for Terry.

Players from rival teams still socialise together, but you can imagine the reaction now if the shot was re-created with players from the top sides in the Premiership. I don't suppose Sir Alex would be too pleased if any of his lads were to appear in the press flanked by brandy glasses and smoking the finest Havanas Cuba has to offer. Now there's an idea...

Just as evocative are the photographs of the fans that appear in this amazing collection. When I was young, I'd be carried to Highbury on my dad's shoulders, and be part of the immense throng that crammed into the North Bank to watch Arsenal. Looking back now, it seems impossible that so many people could fit into grounds that now hold only half as many spectators.

And like most players, that's how I began my love affair with the game: as a supporter. From the age of six, I was kicking a ball around in the streets and dreaming of the day when I'd walk out at Wembley as captain of England. Johnny Haynes was my first hero, and the England captain of the time, but the book is packed with players to whom I looked up, even though some of them were playing at the same time as me.

Jimmy Greaves was probably the greatest goalscorer of all time, and someone whose ability impressed me so much that I actually spent time in training trying to finish like him – I couldn't. Then there was Bobby Moore, a friend and team-mate, and probably the game's first media superstar. He and his first wife Tina were the Posh and Becks of their time: glamorous, fashionable and idolised by people all over the nation. Then there's my old pal George Best, who, along with Pele, remains the most naturally gifted footballer I've ever seen. As the photos here testify, George was a phenomenally good-looking man, and he took over Bobby Moore's mantle as the most photographed British footballer and became an icon. I got to play alongside Bobby and George at Fulham [see right].

There are scores of other players in this book whom I watched and admired, either as a fan or a contemporary, but some of the most powerful images capture those who'd only be recognized by close family. These are the kids who have always been found – as I was – playing down any street, in any playground and on any patch of grass across the country; and the Sunday and lunch-break footballers who are still scoring that last-minute winner in the FA Cup Final.

This book offers many more insights into what the game means to people and its history. Some of the images you'll find here, such as those capturing the construction of Wembley's twin towers and the classic old East Stand at White Hart Lane, tell the story of football's previous boom, when, in the years after the first World War, new stadia sprang up everywhere.

Only in the last five years or so has the game been able to afford a similar rebuilding programme, and I'm sure that in time we'll look back upon the 1990s

and beyond as the start of another golden era. But will these moments be captured in the same way? I doubt it.

Which is why we need a book like this one. It's not, as John says, about the goals, but about what makes the goals important: the charisma of the great players and managers, the passion of the fans, the fact that football will take you from one emotional extreme to the other. All in the space of 90 minutes, as any England fan can tell you. The images collected here bring all of this home, and they make for a unique look back at 85 years of the game.

Which brings me back to another Terry O'Neill photograph: this one was taken in 1972, a few months after 'The Clan' shot and not long after I'd moved from Queens Park Rangers to Manchester City [see page 370]. With top footballers today earning over £100,000 a week, their relationship with the press has changed: while players and press then were friends and drinking companions, nowadays the players feel constantly threatened and hassled. But Terry was able to take a fantastic photograph of myself alongside Geoff Hurst, Gordon Banks, Martin Chivers and a few other familiar faces. And sat right at the centre of it – just where he liked to be – with all eyes on him and every inch 'The Godfather', is my manager at the time, Malcolm Allison.

It's unlikely that photographs such as this one will be taken again. And I doubt you'll see another manager like Malcolm in a hurry. But that's what this book is all about: one-offs. RODNEY MARSH

Sheffield Wednesday supporters. Circa 1940. Photographer not known

West Ham's full-back Jack Burkett undergoes heat-treatment physiotherapy. January 1965. Photograph by Norman Quicke

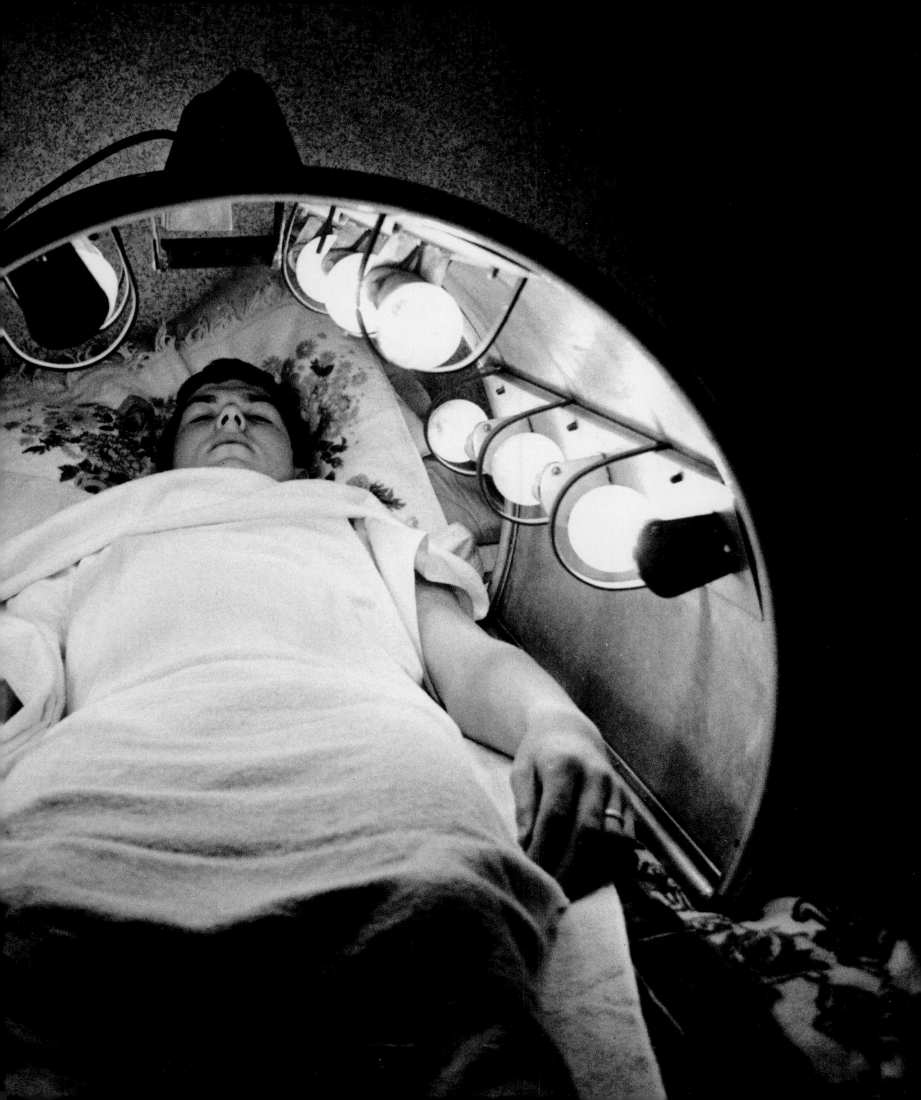

The annual Shrovetide football game
played at Ashbourne, Derbyshire.
March 1960. Photographer not known

Stanley Matthews and family on Blackpool beach.
September 1953. Photograph by Bert Hardy

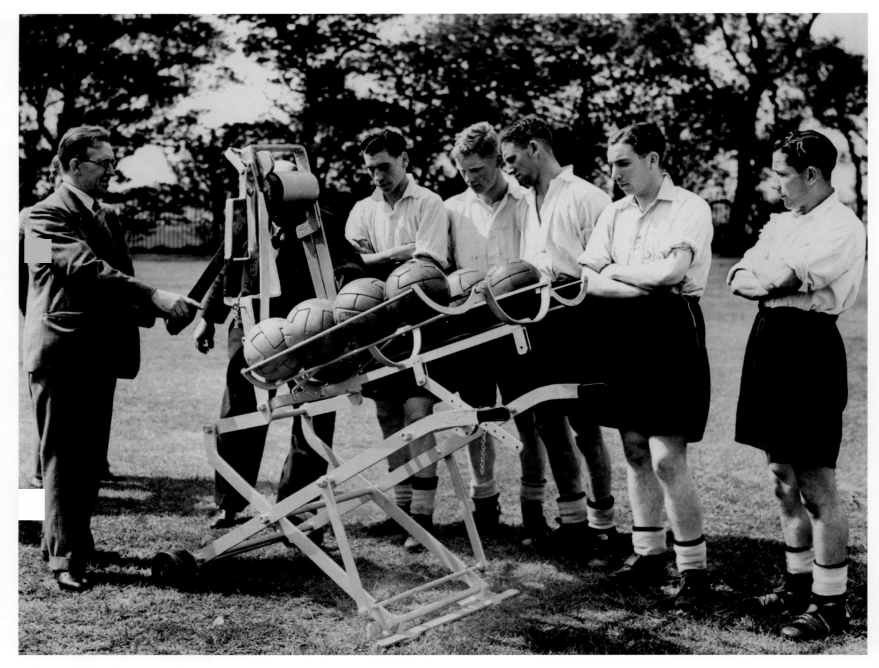

Wolverhampton Wanderers players inspect an automated crossing machine. July 1938. Photographer not known

Opposite: Watford goalkeeper Jim McLaren. January 1938. Photograph by E. Dean

Newpaper sellers on Victoria Embankment, London.
January 1936. Photograph by H.F. Davies

Barnsley equalise but Leicester City go on to win their FA Cup Sixth Round replay 2–1. March 1961. Photograph by Vic Clements

Southern League Yeovil Town beat Sunderland of Division One 2–1 in the Fourth Round of the FA Cup. January 1949. Photographer not known

Tommy Smith of Liverpool. February 1974.
Photograph by Bob Thomas

Opposite: Nobby Stiles of Manchester United.
November 1969. Photograph by Ray Green

Five hundred people watch the FA Cup Final on twenty television sets in Kensington Town Hall, London. Arsenal beat Liverpool 2–0. April 1950. Photograph by E. Round

FIFA president Stanley Rous selects the type of ball to be used in the 1966 World Cup finals. May 1965. Photograph by Robert Stiggins

Opposite: Webbers, the London-based football manufacturer. December 1950. Photographer not known

Harry Rogers of Chalk Farm, London, makes a promise to his customers. But Chelsea go out 1–0 at home to Grimsby in the Sixth Round of the FA Cup. 1939. Photographer not known

Tottenham Hotspur take a preventative gargle against 'flu. January 1933. Photograph by E.E. Haynes

Wolverhampton Wanderers drink malted milk. April 1939. Photograph by Kurt Hutton

The Graf Zeppelin sails over Wembley during the FA Cup Final. Down on the pitch Arsenal beat Huddersfield 2–0. April 1930. Photograph by J. Gaiger. Opposite: photographer not known

Factory workers in
Kilmarnock, Scotland.
October 1955.
Photograph by
Malcolm Dunbar

Sunderland's £100,000 sextet: centre-half Roy Daniel, centre-forward Ted Purdon, outside-right Tom Wright, inside-forward Kenneth Chisholm, left-back William Elliott and outside-right Billy Bingham. February 1954. Photograph by M. Mckeown

Police remove boots and shoes from supporters when Manchester United visit Queens Park Rangers at Loftus Road. September 1975. Photographer not known

Opposite: A ticket tout outside Craven Cottage. February 1958.
Photographer not known

An England squad in club colours. Back row, left to right: Ray Wilson, Everton; Gordon Milne, Liverpool; George Cohen, Fulham; Willie Stevenson, Liverpool; Ron Springett, Sheffield Wednesday; Gordon Banks, Leicester City; Jack Charlton, Leeds United; Geoff Hurst, West Ham United; Peter Thompson, Liverpool; Paul Reaney, Leeds United; Gordon Harris, Burnley; Harold Shepherdson, England trainer.

Front row, left to right: Nobby Stiles, Manchester United; Norman Hunter, Leeds United; Keith Newton, Blackburn Rovers; Joe Baker, Arsenal; Alan Ball, Blackpool; Bobby Moore, West Ham United; Jimmy Greaves, Tottenham Hotspur; George Eastham, Arsenal; Ron Flowers, Wolverhampton Wanderers; Bobby Charlton, Manchester United. Spring 1966. Photographer not known

Littlewood pools winners. 1930s. Photographers not known

Ipswich Town players after a 2–1 defeat at home to Aston Villa in their Third Round FA Cup replay. January 1939. Photographer not known

Preceding pages: A downpour at Craven Cottage. 1965. Photographer not known

Portsmouth supporter. April 1934. Photographer not known

Opposite: West Bromwich Albion supporter. April 1935.
Photograph by S.C. Smith

A British Army XI plays
an international team,
comprising two Belgians,
two Dutchmen, two Poles,
two Norwegians and
three Czechoslovakians,
at Stamford Bridge,
March 1941. Photograph
by Bert Hardy

Bobby Moore after West Ham United win the FA Cup Final, May 1964. Photograph by Kent Gavin

Opposite: Modelling Hardy Amies for a 'Daily Express' fashion shoot, 1966. Photograph by M. McKeown

Houses in Paxton Road are demolished to make way for a new stand at White Hart Lane. May 1936. Photograph by Martin

Opposite: The Clock End, Highbury. August 1930. Photographer not known

Pupils of St Joseph's College train with professional coach George Smith. October 1948. Photographs by George Konig

Opposite: The start of the Restaurant Junior Charity Cup Final at
Highbury, April 1929. Photograph by Puttnam

Edward, Prince of Wales, kicks off a friendly between Tottenham
Hotspur and Fulham after inspecting the Champion Cadet Battalion
at Sandhurst, 1921. Photographer not known

Frank Swift,
Manchester City's
goalkeeper, also
works as a public
relations officer
for a catering firm.
January 1948.
Photograph by
Charles Hewitt

Chelsea training before their Sixth Round FA Cup tie against Liverpool. February 1932. Photographer not known

Wrexham training in the run-up to their Fourth Round FA Cup tie against Manchester United. January 1957. Photographer not known

West Ham United supporters arrive at Wembley for the first FA Cup Final to be played at the national stadium; their team loses 2–0 to Bolton Wanderers in front of an estimated crown of 200,000. April 1923. Photographer not known

Frankie Vaughan leads the singing at Wembley before the FA Cup Final between Leeds United and Sunderland. May 1973. Photographer not known

Opposite: FA Cup Final crowd control at Wembley for Arsenal versus Sheffield United. April 1936. Photographer not known

Bob Paisley in Liverpool's sponsor's colours at Anfield. May 1982. Photographer not known

Opposite: Leaving the pitch with the Division One Championship trophy after his last home game in charge of Liverpool. May 1983. Photographer not known

Kickabout, Purley Way, London. January 1969.
Photographer not known

Opposite: Torquay United train on the beach at Anstey's Cove.
February 1938. Photograph by Reg Speller

Overleaf, left: Plymouth Argyle supporters. January 1922.
Photographer not known

Overleaf, right: Arsenal supporters. February 1936.
Photograph by Hudson

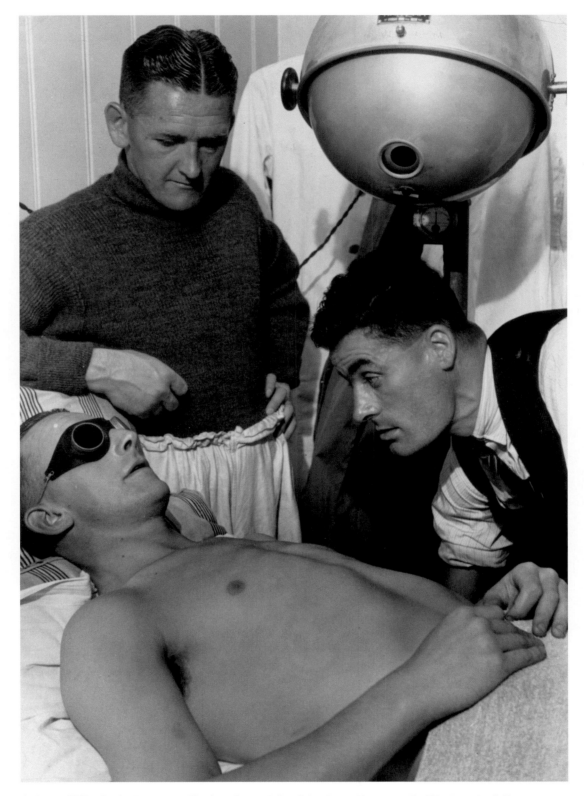

Johnny O'Harte looks on as Chelsea's assistant trainer, Norman Smith, treats fellow full-back Jacky Smith. August 1939. Photograph by Kurt Hutton

Opposite: Buxton Town's centre-half, Joe Wilson, enjoys a high-pressure shower massage. December 1951. Photograph by Hicklin

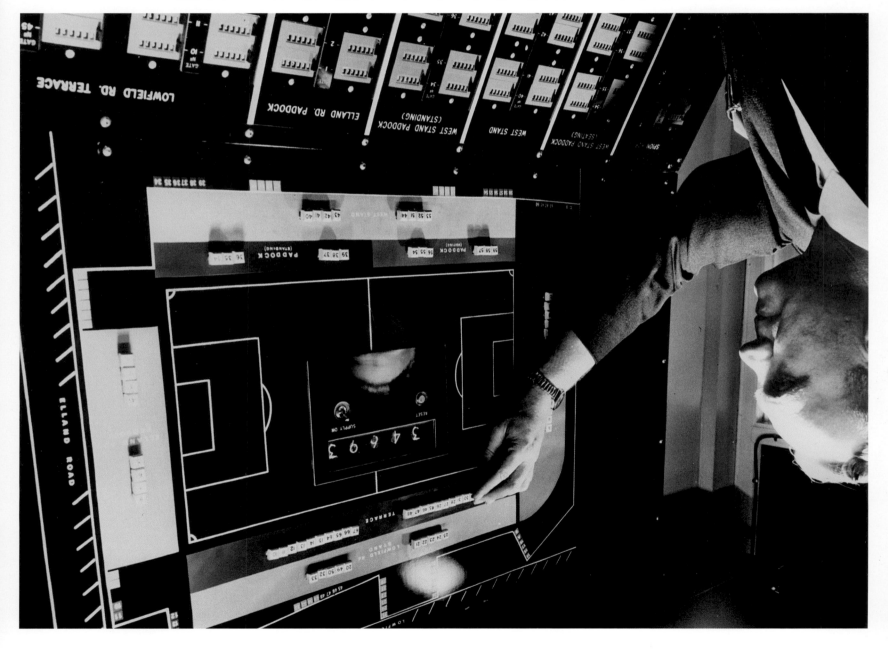

Leeds United's Electronic Summation System, on which the attendance in each part of Elland Road is recorded. 1950s.
Photographer not known

Workmen assemble seating at Wembley in last-minute preparation for the World Cup finals. July 1966. Photograph by Chris Barham

Goldie the golden eagle,
escapee from London Zoo,
perches in Regent's Park.
December 1965.
Photographer not known

Bolton Wanderers are on their way to Wembley for
the FA Cup Final against Manchester City. April 1926.
Photographer not known

Maldon Ladies Football Club, formed for a charity match, walk out for their ninety-fifth game. November 1953. Photograph by Peter Waugh
Opposite: Brenda Chittenden, goalkeeper for East Kent Packers. November 1953. Photographer not known

Walsall secretary Ernest Wilson entertains the crowd at
Fellows Park, December 1952. Photograph by R. Saidman

Opposite: The Remote Control Telesonic Apparatus
makes one-to-one coaching possible, January 1949.
Photographer not known

West Ham United supporters at an
FA Cup Semi-final against Everton; their
team loses 2–1. March 1933. Photographer
not known

George Best is carried off injured. March 1969. Photographer not known

Opposite: In the bath at Old Trafford. 1967. Photograph by Ray Green

Warren Mitchell, as Alf Garnett, at Upton Park. February 1968. Photographer not known

Opposite: Wolverhampton Wanderers supporter. March 1949. Photograph by Charles Hewitt

The Arsenal squad trains
on the A6. July 1962.
Photographer not known

Preceding pages: The
home dressing-room at
Highbury. November 1938.
Photograph by H.F. Davies

Walthamstow Schoolboys after beating West Ham Schoolboys 3–1. January 1931. Photograph by A.R. Coster

Kickabout in London. 1962. Photographer not known

The Crazy Gang act as stretcher bearers at the
annual charity match between boxers and jockeys;
this year's game is played at The Den. October 1936.
Photograph by Ward

Colchester United play Norwich City. October 1950. Photograph by John Chillingworth

Opposite: The Colchester supporters' registration hut. October 1950. Photograph by M. McKeown

Wing-half Frank Houghton and goalkeeper Jack Fairbrother with Newcastle United's trainer Norman Smith. August 1948.
Photographer not known

Opposite: Portsmouth's kit-man Bill Wright. December 1952.
Photograph by R. Saidman

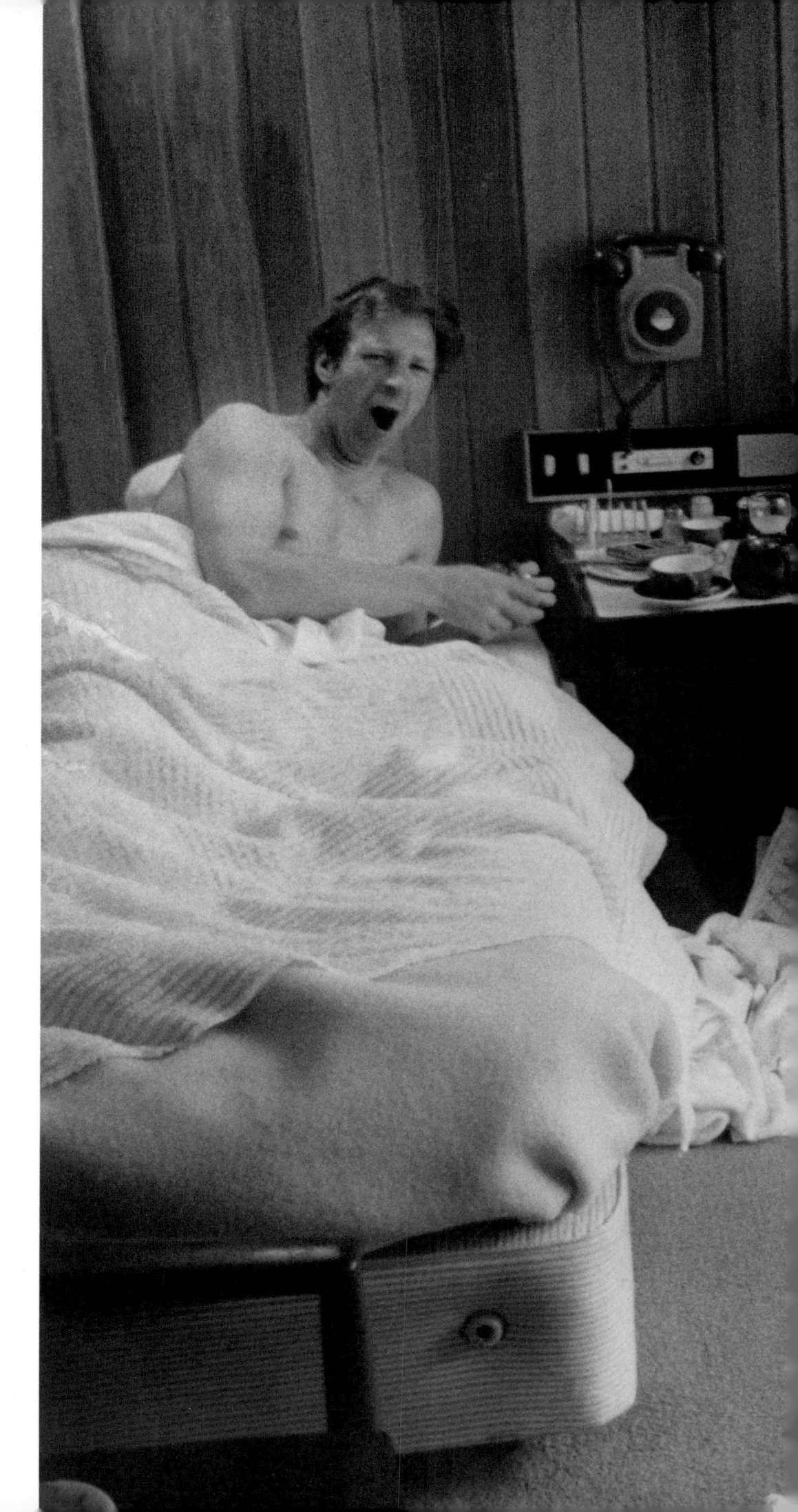

Jack Charlton and Billy Bremner share a room
for a Leeds United away game. May 1972.
Photograph by Henson

Tottenham Hotspur supporters protest the allocation of FA Cup Final tickets in Trafalgar Square.
Spurs and Burnley are to receive 15,000 tickets each. April 1962. Photographer not known

Opposite: Wembley box office staff load tickets for posting. March 1945. Photographer not known

Jimmy Greaves at a Tottenham Hotspur photo-call.
April 1962. Photographer not known

Opposite: Centre-half Sidney Plackett at a Notts County
photo-call. August 1929. Potographer not known

Kickabout, Salford. May 1955. Photograph by Salt

Kickabout, London. August 1933. Photographer not known

Three thousand bales of straw are laid at White Hart Lane to protect the pitch from frost. December 1925. Photograph by Davis

Opposite: Ground staff at Stoke City attempt to thaw the ground. Stanley Matthews warms his hands over one of the braziers. December 1938. Photographer not known

Fulham and Blackpool players observe two minutes' silence for King George V before
the Fourth Round FA Cup tie at Craven Cottage. January 1936. Photographer not known

Opposite: A minute's silence for President Kennedy before Fulham play Sheffield United.
November 1963. Photograph by Douglas Miller

Fred Packham, plater and polisher, on the day before the FA Cup Final. The cup is lifted by Roy Paul, captain of the Manchester City team that beats Birmingham City 3-1. May 1956. Photograph by Douglas Miller

Opposite: D. Wiseman and R.H. Brough draw Millwall at home to Tottenham Hotspur in the Third Round of the FA Cup. January 1967. Photographer not known

Nigeria's inside forward Ebenezer prepares for a match against Bishop Auckland during his country's goodwill tour of Britain. 1950. Photograph by Charles Hewitt

Opposite: The Nigeria team wear support straps but not boots. Photograph by Charles Hewitt

Following page: Sheffield United supporters in the Mall before the FA Cup Final. April 1936. Photograph by Allen

Tommy Docherty takes Chelsea on holiday to Cannes after winning the Second Division Championship. July 1963. Photographer not known

Following pages: Cardiff City versus Chelsea at Ninian Park. March 1921. Photograph by Arthur R. Coster

Alf Ramsey prevents George Cohen from swapping shirts after England beat Argentina in the Quarter-final of the World Cup. July 1966.
Photographer not known

Preceding pages, left: Arsenal's centre-forward Ted Drake dons a shinpad. January 1938.
Photographer not known

Preceding pages, right: The 'Tornado', designed by former referee Englebert K. Harmer of Vienna, who explains 'The boot has no laces but is held fast to the foot by a rubber strap with rings on both sides of the heel. It is much lighter than a conventional boot and has a rubber padded instep with a "Special Kicking Pad" just beneath.' March 1958.
Photographer not known

Wembley ground staff prepare the flagpole before the first
FA Cup Final. The national stadium had taken 300 days to
build and was completed four days before the Final. April 1923.
Photographer not known

Opposite: One of Wembley's 'twin towers' under construction.
1923. Photographer not known

Tottenham Hotspur players take a brine bath at
Southend-on-Sea. January 1936. Photograph by Allen

Opposite: Centre-forward Jack Rowley of Manchester
United. February 1948. Photograph by William Vanderson

Half-back Arthur Grimsdell of Tottenham Hotspur parades the FA Cup, won with a 1–0 victory over Wolverhampton Wanderers (the Final was played at Stamford Bridge), down the High Road. April 1921. Photographer not known

Opposite: Spurs return the FA Cup to Football Association headquarters. February 1963. Photograph by Reg Lancaster

Chelsea goalkeeper Harry Medhurst coaching at Beverley School, New Malden, London. October 1949. Photographer not known

Opposite: Ten-year-old Billy Neil of Glasgow emigrating to Australia. October 1947. Photograph by Graham Hales

Littlewoods pools winner Keith Nicholson of Castleford, Yorkshire, is presented with a cheque for £152,319 by Bruce Forsyth. September 1961. Photograph by Ron Case

Opposite: Viv Nicholson, recently separated from husband Keith, with her £2,500 Chevrolet Impala. March 1962. Photographer not known

Bolton Wanderers players with Roy Pilkington, who has walked 195 miles from Bolton to Wembley to watch his team play Manchester United in the FA Cup Final. May 1958. Photographer not known

Opposite: Nottingham Forest return home with the FA Cup having beaten Luton Town 2–1. May 1959. Photographer not known

Brentford manager Jackie Gibbons commentates
for blind supporters, who are admitted free and
provided with headphones by the club. August 1951.
Photographer not known

Cardiff City's Len Davis demonstrates his reach. 1921.
Photographer not known

Opposite: Chlesea's new signing, Alex Stepney, watches his goalkeeping rival, Peter Bonetti, in training. August 1966.
Photographer not known

Spectators at Crystal Palace. April 1914.
Photographer not known

149

Everton supporters model 'weather-beaters' in the club's colours before the FA Cup Final against West Bromwich Albion. May 1968. Photographer not known

Opposite: Bristol Rovers supporters. February 1958. Photograph by Terry Fincher

Newly developed plastic footballs are claimed to be tougher than the traditional leather ball. April 1952. Photographer not known

Constructing covered terracing
at The Valley. February 1934.
Photograph by Reg Speller

A ball-propelling machine tests centre-forwards, defenders and goalkeepers at Highbury. January 1950. Photographer not known

Stan Lynn of Birmingham City works on his shooting skills. January 1965. Photograph by R. Viner

A cameraman at Wembley films the FA Cup Final between
Sheffield Wednesday and West Bromwich Albion. April 1935.
Photographer not known

Opposite: Gaumont British Picture Corporation film schoolboy
football for a newsreel. April 1935. Photograph by Harry Todd

Deaf-and-dumb players from England and Wales
toss up. The Wales captain calls 'heads'. September 1925.
Photograph by Brooke

Opposite: Arsenal versus Manchester United at Highbury.
January 1926. Photograph by H.F. Davis

Hornsey YMCA on the rooftop of their clubhouse. September 1936.
Photograph by Fred Morley

Opposite: Saint Joseph's Academy, Blackheath, take down the goalposts after a game. February 1957. Photograph not known

Following pages: Hackney Marshes, London. October 1962.
Photographer not known

Left-half Wilf Copping of Arsenal. August 1934. Photograph by Fred Morley

Opposite: Goalkeeper Nigel Sims of Wolverhampton Wanderers. November 1952. Photograph by Charles Hewitt

The cast of 'Cuckoo in the Nest' backstage
at the Aldwych Theatre, London.
December 1925. Photographer not known

Kickabout in an empty dry dock at the Royal Albert Docks, London.
April 1931. Photographer not known

Opposite: Break time kickabout beneath the bows of the QE2, nearing
completion at the John Brown shipyard, Clydebank. September 1967.
Photographer not known

Norman Wisdom introduces the new club song to the crowd at Brighton and Hove Albion's Goldstone Ground. March 1965. Photographer not known

Opposite: Non-league Peterborough United, the night before their Second Round FA Cup tie against Swindon Town of Division Three South, visit the Prince of Wales Theatre, London, where they meet Ilona Adams and Tommy Cooper. December 1955. Photographer not known

Plymouth Argyle fans release their lucky balloon before a First Round
FA Cup tie against Notts County. January 1923. Photographer not known

Arsenal supporters at Highbury.
December 1951. Photograph by
George Douglas

Wounded soldiers at Blenheim Palace. 1916. Photographer not known

Disabled ex-servicemen attend a garden party at Buckingham Palace. July 1953. Photographer not known

Terry Venables at Stamford Bridge after being
dropped from the Chelsea team. April 1965.
Photograph by David Cairns

The Boleyn Ground, Upton Park. March 1930.
Photograph by S.R. Gaiger

Bolton Wanderers' Nat Lofthouse recuperates with his family following an operation on an injury picked up while playing Tottenham Hotspur. March 1958. Photographer not known

Opposite: An X-ray of Lofthouse's shoulder after surgery.

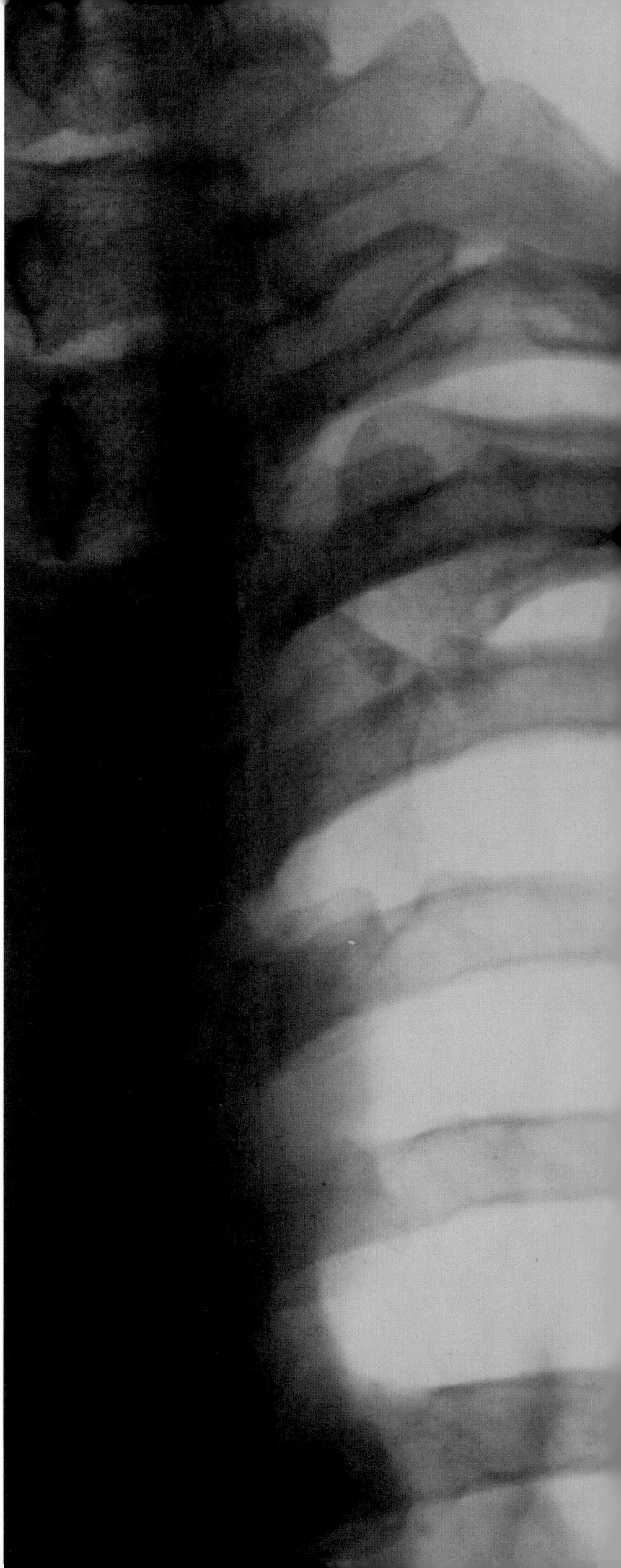

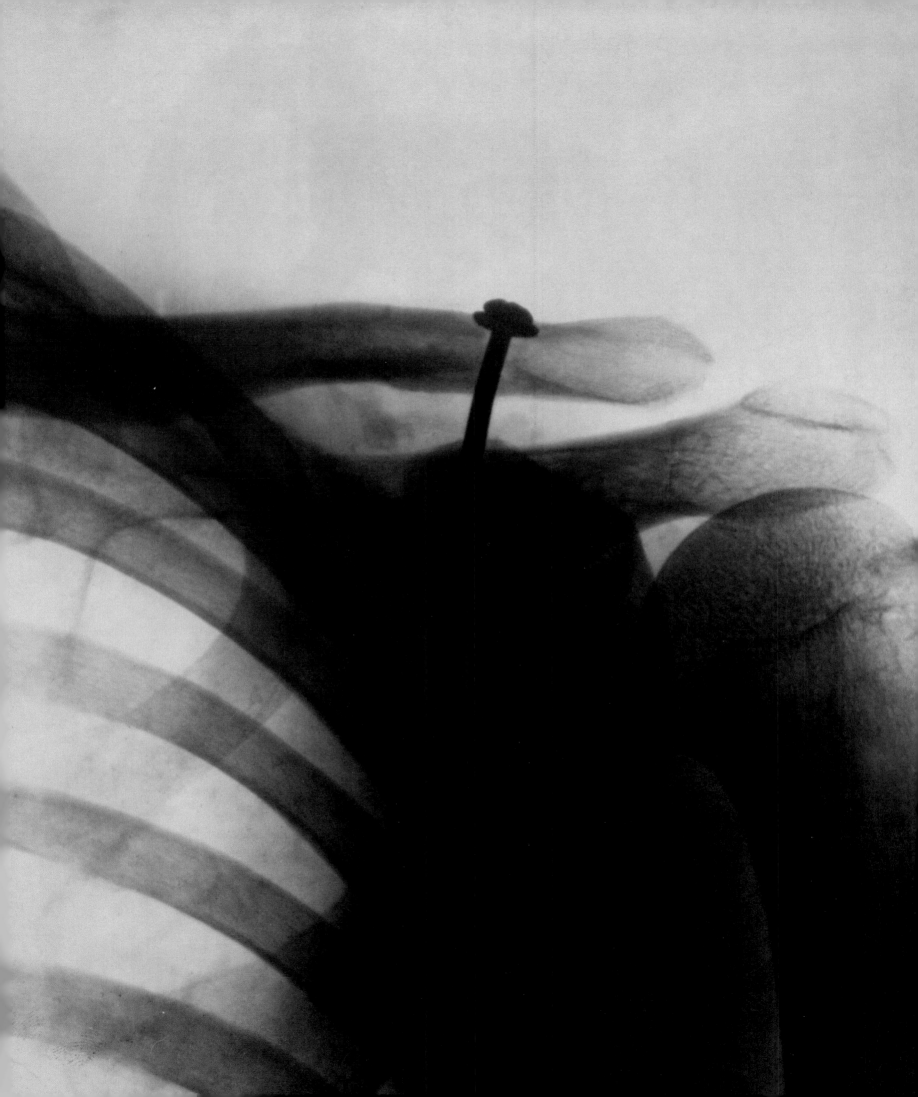

Captain and centre-half Jimmy Seddon, goalkeeper Dick Pym and centre-forward Harry Blackmore of Bolton Wanderers, the day after they beat Portsmouth 2–0 in the FA Cup Final. April 1929. Photographer not known

Bolton Wanderers manager Bill Ridding holds the FA Cup as Nat Lofthouse, captain of the side that beat Manchester United 2–0, takes a celebratory drink. May 1958. Photographer not known

The Tottenham cockerel is cleaned while White Hart Lane is enlarged, adding 25,000 to the capacity. July 1934. Photograph by R. Wesley

Opposite: The new stand under construction. July 1934. Photograph by H.F. Davis

Preceding pages: Arsenal supporters at Highbury. December 1951. Photograph by George Douglas

The annual mud-football game at the Leigh-on-Sea regatta. August 1925. Photograph by Brooke

Cliff Bastin, who scored 150 League goals for Arsenal, at home in Edgware after retiring from the game. 1948.
Photographer not known

Manager Bob Stokoe and captain Bobby Kerr, after Sunderland's 1–0 victory over Leeds United in the FA Cup Final. May 1973. Photograph by Douglas Miller

Opposite: An Everton supporter grabs the FA Cup from left winger Derek Temple, who scored the winner against Sheffield Wednesday. May 1966. Photographer not known

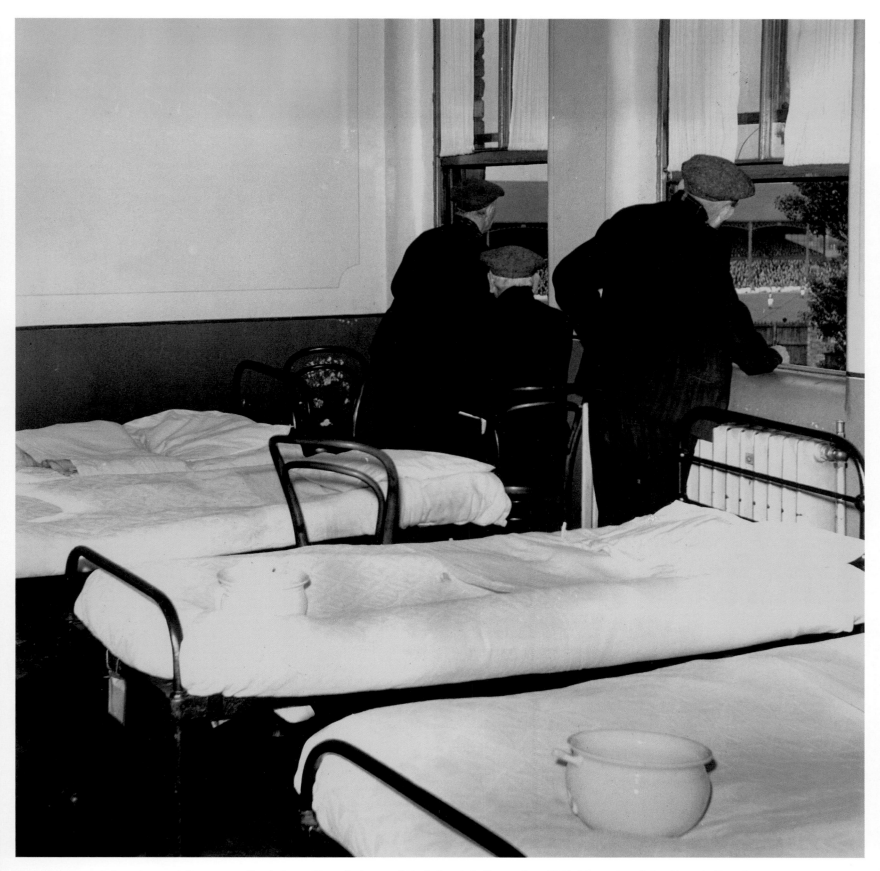

Pensioners watch a game at Ayresome Park from the windows of their hostel. November 1951. Photograph by George Douglas
Opposite: A lockout at Carrow Road for Norwich City's game against Portsmouth. January 1950. Photograph by F. Greaves

Spurs parade through Tottenham after beating Burnley 3–1 in the FA Cup Final. May 1962. Photograph by Douglas Miller

Opposite: On the open-top bus, Spurs players' sons Stephen Smith and Richard Blanchflower hold the cup. May 1962. Photographer not known

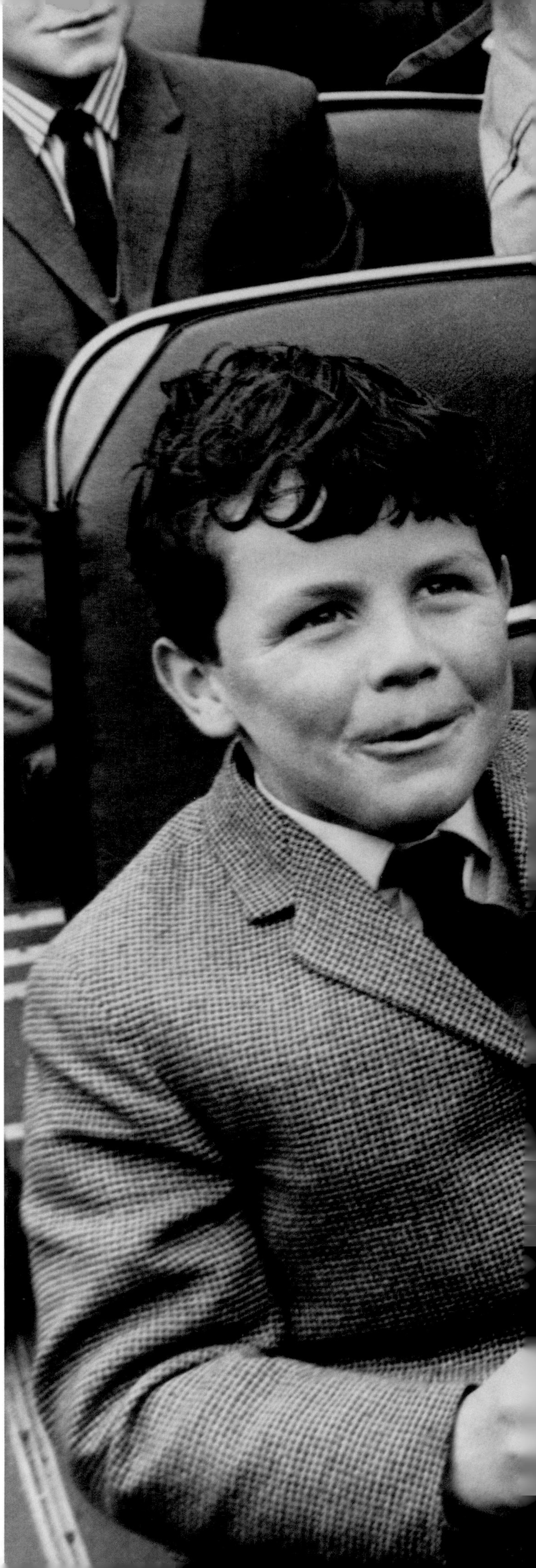

A Grimsby Town supporter waves a lucky cod mascot as the team run out. March 1939. Photograph by David Savill

Alf Ramsey meets managers of northern teams. Back row, left to right: Trevor Porteous, player–manager of Stockport County; Les MacDowall, Oldham Athletic; Ronnie Suart, Blackpool; Harry Potts, Burnley; Jimmy Milne, Preston North End; Matt Busby, Manchester United; Harry Catterick, Everton; Don Revie, Leeds United; George Poyser, Manchester City;

Johnny Harris, Sheffield United. Front row, left to right: Stan Whitehorn, Football Association; Ike Robinson, Football Association; Alf Ramsey; Alan Brown, Sheffield Wednesday; Jack Marshall, Blackburn; John Carey, Nottingham Forest; Dave Russell, Tranmere Rovers. October 1964. Photographer not known

A Sunday washout in Essex. September 1926.
Photograph by H.F. Davis

Jackie Charlton on the pitch at Elland Road, where the ice is two inches thick. Leeds United say there is a '50-50' chance the cup-tie against Stoke can be played, but the match is eventually postponed for two months. January 1963. Photographer not known

Opposite: Liverpool's Kevin Keegan and Leeds United's Billy Bremner are sent off for fighting during the Charity Shield match at Wembley. August 1974. Photograph by Robert Stiggins

Preceding pages, left:
Programme seller
at Stamford Bridge.
February 1949.
Photograph by
Chris Ware

Preceding pages,
right: Wolverhampton
Wanderers fans
locked out of the FA
Cup semi-final replay
against Manchester
United at Goodison
Park. April 1949.
Photograph by
Charles Hewitt

Bobby and Tina
Moore, Epping
Forest. March 1966.
Photograph by
Terry O'Neill

213

Ticketless Newcastle United supporters outside Wembley while their team play – and lose to – Liverpool in the FA Cup Final. May 1974. Photograph by Bart Leddy

Opposite: A Manchester United supporter climbs into Wembley for the European Cup Final against Benfica. May 1968. Photograph by Ron Case

Ballet teacher Yvonne Burr takes Ronald Peters, captain of Littlehampton Boys' Club, through his positions. The team win their first game after the new training 17-0. 1955. Photographer not known

Arsenal players leave for Germany to play against service teams. August 1945. Photographer not known

Army sergeants Joe Mercer of Everton, Matt Busby of Liverpool and Don Welsh of Charlton Athletic. 1939. Photographer not known

FA Cup holders Wolverhampton
Wanderers take the trophy
to their Third Round tie at
Plymouth Argyle. January 1950.
Photographer not known

The boot-room at Charlton Athletic. August 1936. Photograph by A. Hudson

Opposite: Collecting kit for the laundry at Highbury. October 1947. Photographer not known

Supporters queue for tickets to see Arsenal play a friendly against Dynamo Moscow at White Hart Lane. Highbury is still requisitioned for Air Raid Precaution work. May 1945. Photograph by William Vanderson

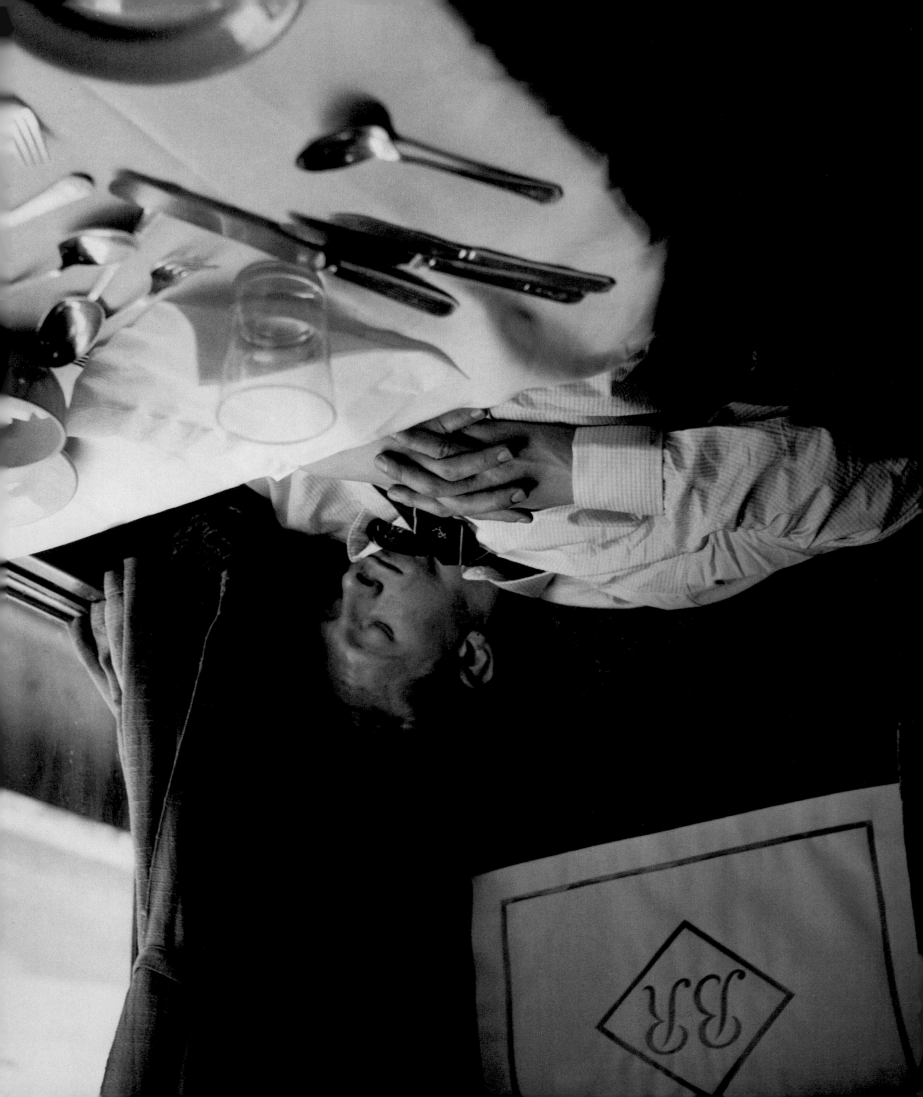

A supporter with Denis Law after Scotland beat England 3–2 at Wembley. The Scots are the first team to defeat Alf Ramsey's side since they won the World Cup the previous year. April 1967. Photographer not known

Opposite: Law asleep on the train home after Manchester United beat Leicester City 3–1 to win the FA Cup. May 1963. Photographer not known

Street game, London.
April 1950.
Photograph by Bill Brandt

Amos the donkey, Barnsley's mascot. 1910. Photographer not known

Opposite: A Notts County supporter at their First Round FA Cup tie away
to Queens Park Rangers. January 1923. Photographer not known

Manchester City take high tea
with the Lord Mayor at the Town
Hall, having beaten Portsmouth
2–1 to win the FA Cup. May 1934.
Photographer not known

GREEN ROVER tickets for a
day's unlimited travel on most
green Country Buses—1500 miles
of London's countryside.
Any day.

Mon.-Fri. after 9.30 a.m.—all day Sats., Suns. and
Bank Holidays—from conductors on green
Country Buses. Not available on Green Line Coaches.

GREEN ROVERS

EVERY
6
(childre

West Ham United's manager Ron Greenwood takes the FA Cup back to Upton Park on the underground. He and the team have been up to London's West End to watch a cinema screening of highlights of their victory over Preston North End. May 1964.
Photographer not known

Preceding pages: A wreath is placed on board the plane bringing home the victims of the Munich aircrash. February 1958.
Photographer not known

England and Wolverhampton Wanderers captain Billy Wright with his landlady, Mrs Colley. 1950.
Photographer not known

Opposite: Arriving home from the 1958 World Cup to be met by Joy (his fiancée), Babs and Teddy
of the Beverley Sisters. June 1958. Photographer not known

Chelsea coach Dave Sexton demonstrates tactics during pre-season training. July 1963.
Photographer not known

Opposite: Leicester City players take lunch together at the club twice a week to help boost
team spirit. March 1949. Photograph by W. Jones

Arsenal parade the FA Cup outside
Islington Town Hall after beating
Huddersfield 2–0 in the final. April 1930.
Photographer not known

242

Middlesbrough's inside-forward Wilf Mannion in training. August 1952. Photographer not known

Opposite: Centre-forward Don Revie, suspended by Manchester City for missing training, keeps himself fit in a local park. August 1955. Photographer not known

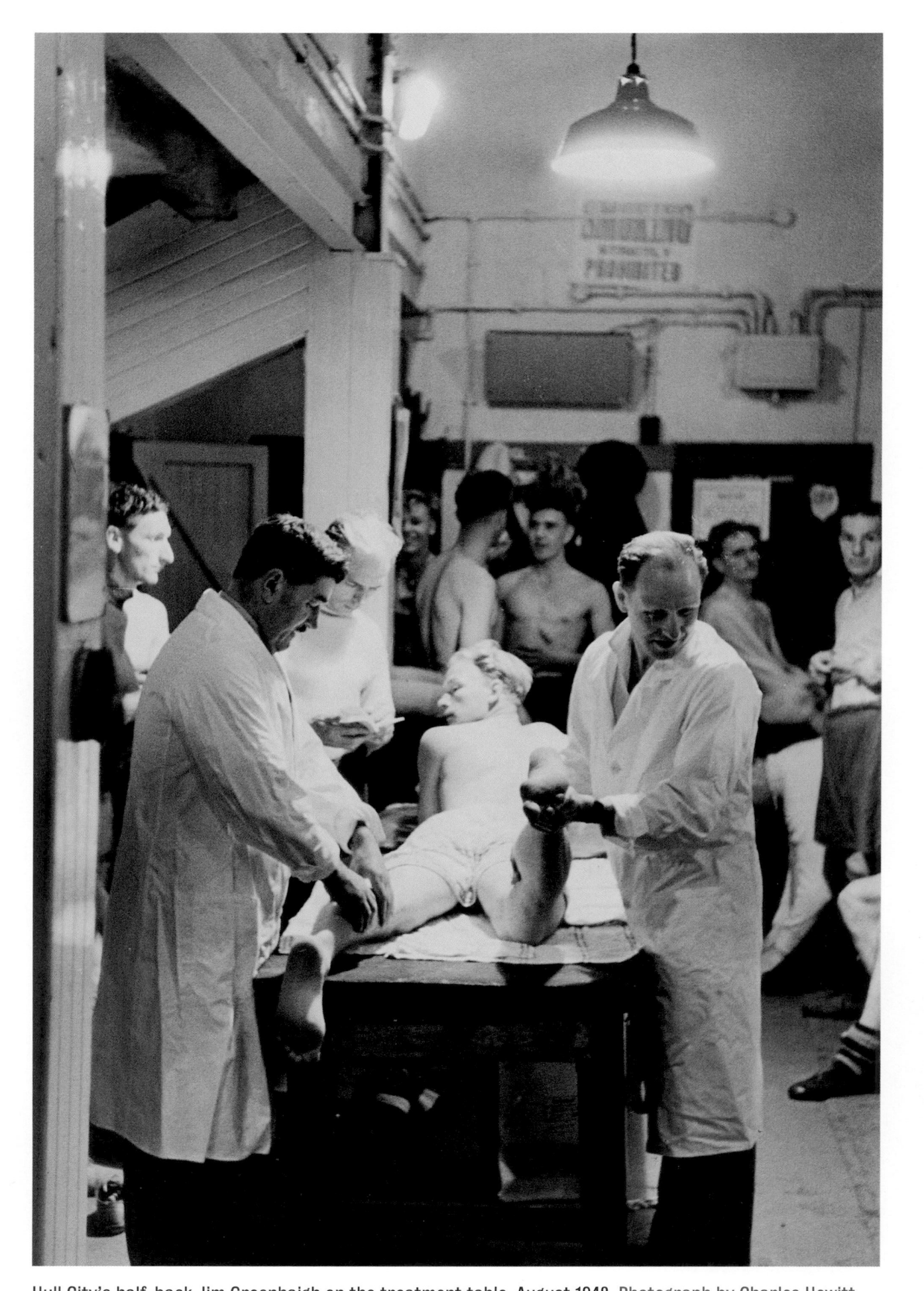

Hull City's half-back Jim Greenhaigh on the treatment table. August 1948. Photograph by Charles Hewitt

Opposite: Manchester City trainer Laurie Barnett with half-back Billy Walsh and inside-forward Spencer Evans in the dressing-room at Maine Road. February 1951. Photograph by John Chillingworth

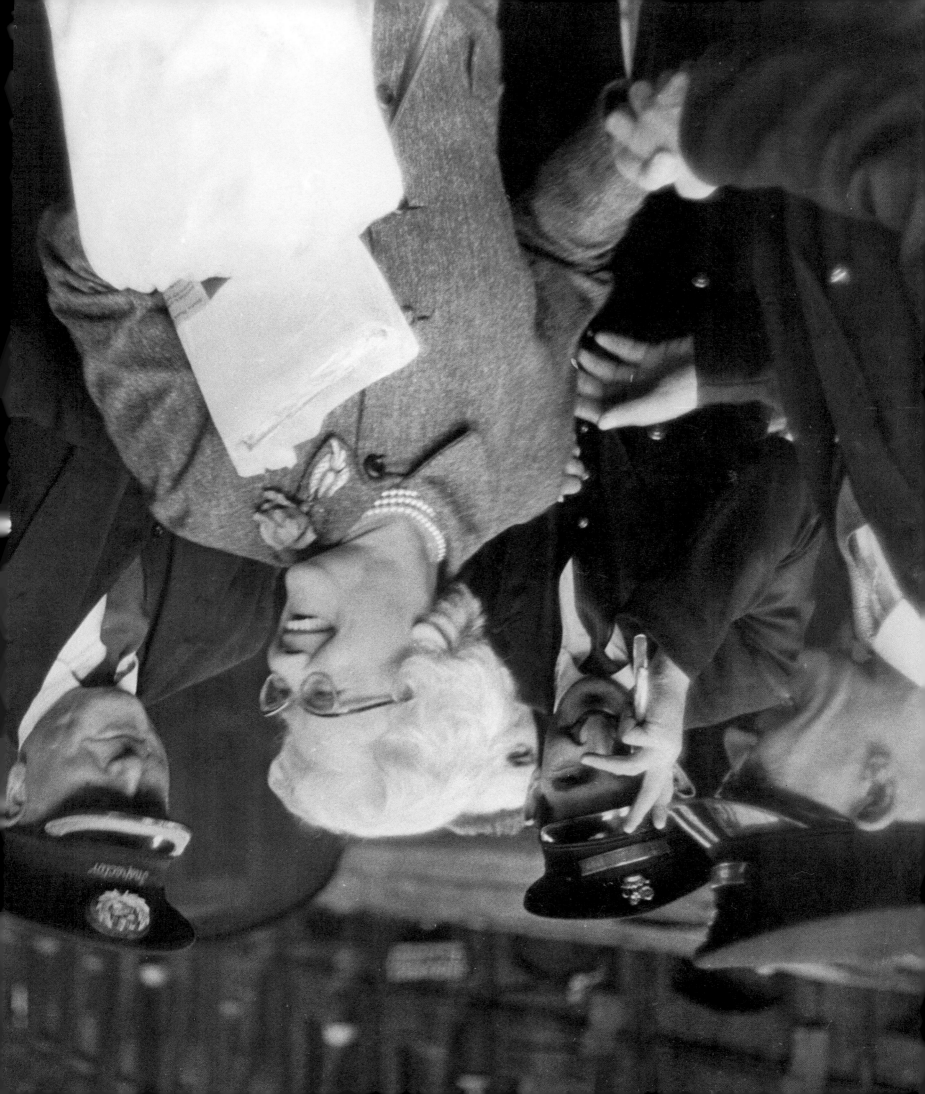

The Queen demonstrates her skill at table football during a
visit to the British Industries Fair at Olympia, London. May 1955.
Photographer not known

Opposite: Cissie Charlton arrives at Kings Cross station, London,
on the way to see her sons Bobby and Jackie play against West
Germany in the World Cup Final. July 1966. Photographer not known

Willie Waddell, Glasgow Rangers' right winger, at home with his son, 1950s. Photographer not known

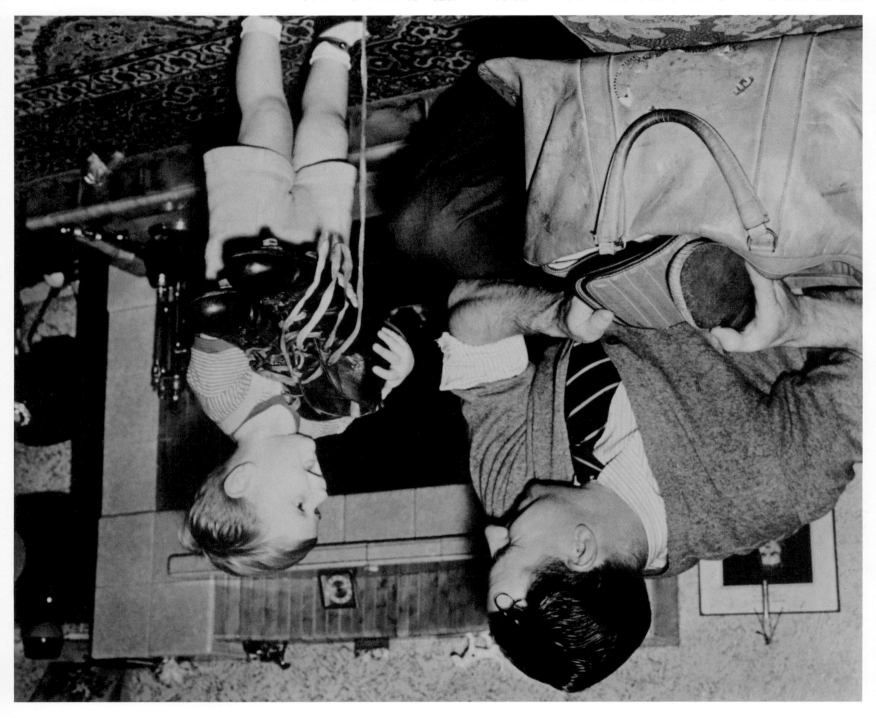

Ally McLeod, Hibernian's left winger, at home with his dog. January 1962. Photographer not known

Blackpool supporters in London to see their team play Fulham in the Sixth Round of the FA Cup. February 1948. Photographer not known

Opposite: 'Ye Silent Twins': Manchester City supporters wear the outfits that won them first prize at Blackpool carnival. They are in London for the FA Cup Final against Bolton Wanderers. April 1926. Photograph by H.F. Davis

Joe Fagan in Rome with the European Cup, the morning after Liverpool beat Roma 4–2 on penalties. May 1984. **Photograph by John Dawes**

The annual football game
played in Atherstone,
Warwickshire, February 1914.
Photographer not known

Tottenham Hotspur before a charity match against a Variety Artists team. March 1923. Photographer not known

The Germany team before they play England in a friendly at White Hart Lane. England win 3–0. December 1935. Photographer not known

Chelsea manager Dave Sexton outside Stamford Bridge. October 1967. Photographer not known

Opposite: West Ham United defender Ken Brown and Chelsea midfielder Terry Venables visit Banham Road in Dagenham, where both were born. January 1965.
Photograph by Norman Quicke

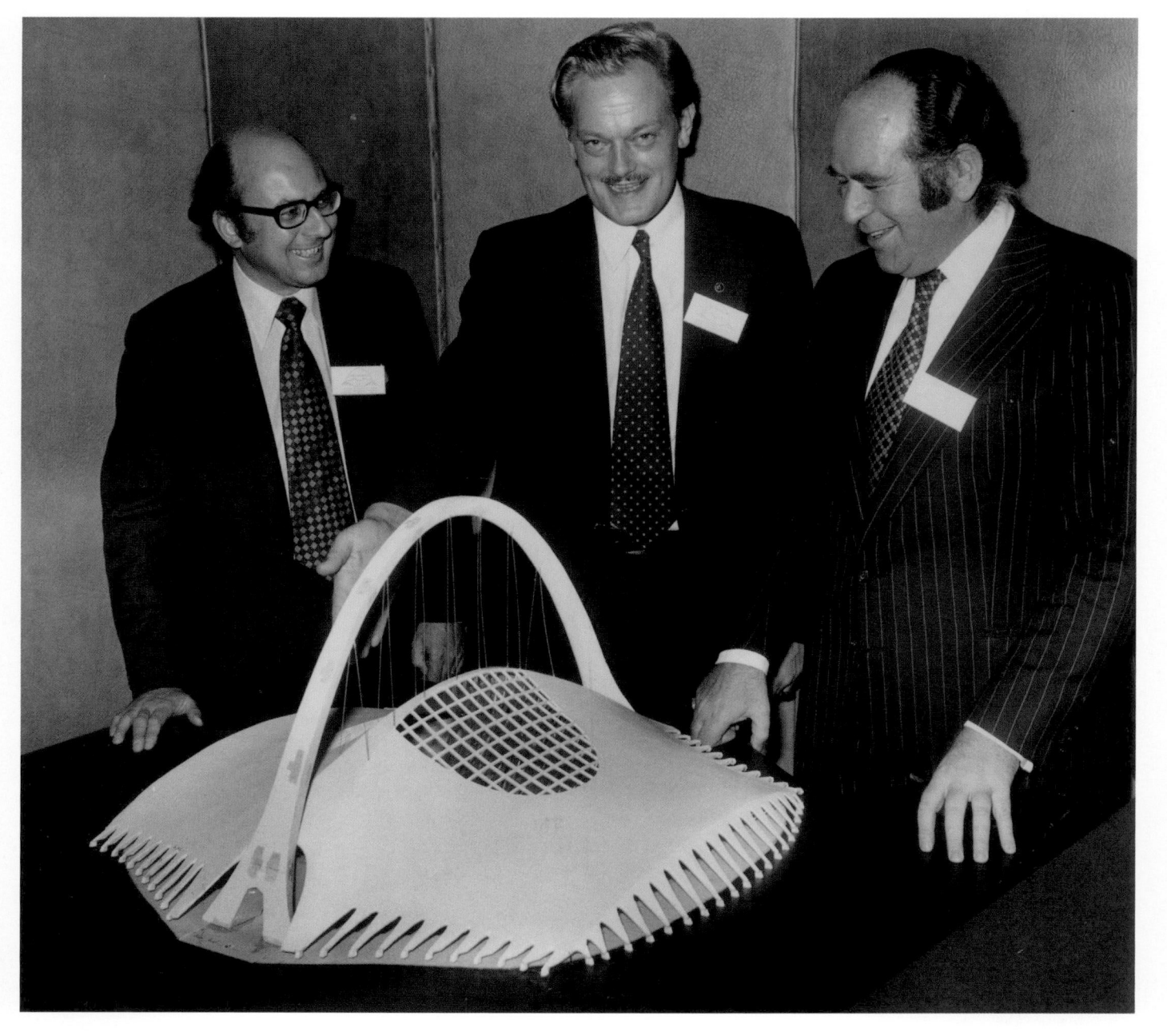

British architects, Ian Fraser, Ray Crownshaw and John Roberts with their design for a football stadium commissioned by the Saudi Arabian royal family. September 1976. Photograph by Roger Jackson

Opposite: The finishing touches are put to the 80lb cake made to celebrate Southampton's fiftieth anniversary. November 1935. Photograph by E. Philips

Ernie Allan, sales manager of stamp dealers Stanley Gibbons, takes delivery of the Jules Rimet trophy at Central Hall, Westminster, London, where it will be displayed at the National Stamp Exhibition. March 1966. Photographer not known

Opposite: Pickles, the dog who found the World Cup, while out for his bedtime walk in Norwood, London, after it had been stolen from the National Stamp Exhibition. March 1966. Photographer not known

Everton supporters arrive at Euston station; they are on the way to see their team play Arsenal at Highbury in a Fourth Round FA Cup tie. Arsenal win 4–3. January 1928. Photograph by H. F. Davis

Following pages: Supporters rush to the White Hart Lane box office to buy tickets to see Tottenham Hotspur against Glasgow Rangers in the Second Round of the European Cup Winners Cup. October 1962. Photograph by Tony Eyles

Above and opposite: Annual Shrovetide football match, Ashbourne, Derbyshire. March 1952. Photographs by Bert Hardy

An Old Boys game at Harrow public school. October 1919. Photograph by Roper

Luton Town supporters on the way to their FA Cup Final against Nottingham Forest. May 1959. Photographer not known

Paul McCartney arrives at Wembley to see Everton play West Bromwich Albion in the FA Cup Final.
May 1968. Photographer not known

Opposite: Rod Stewart on the terraces to see Scotland versus England at Hampden Park. May 1974.
Photograph by D. Morrison

Rod Stewart leaves Hampden
Park after watching Scotland
beat England 2–0 in the Home
Championship. May 1974.
Photograph by D. Morrison

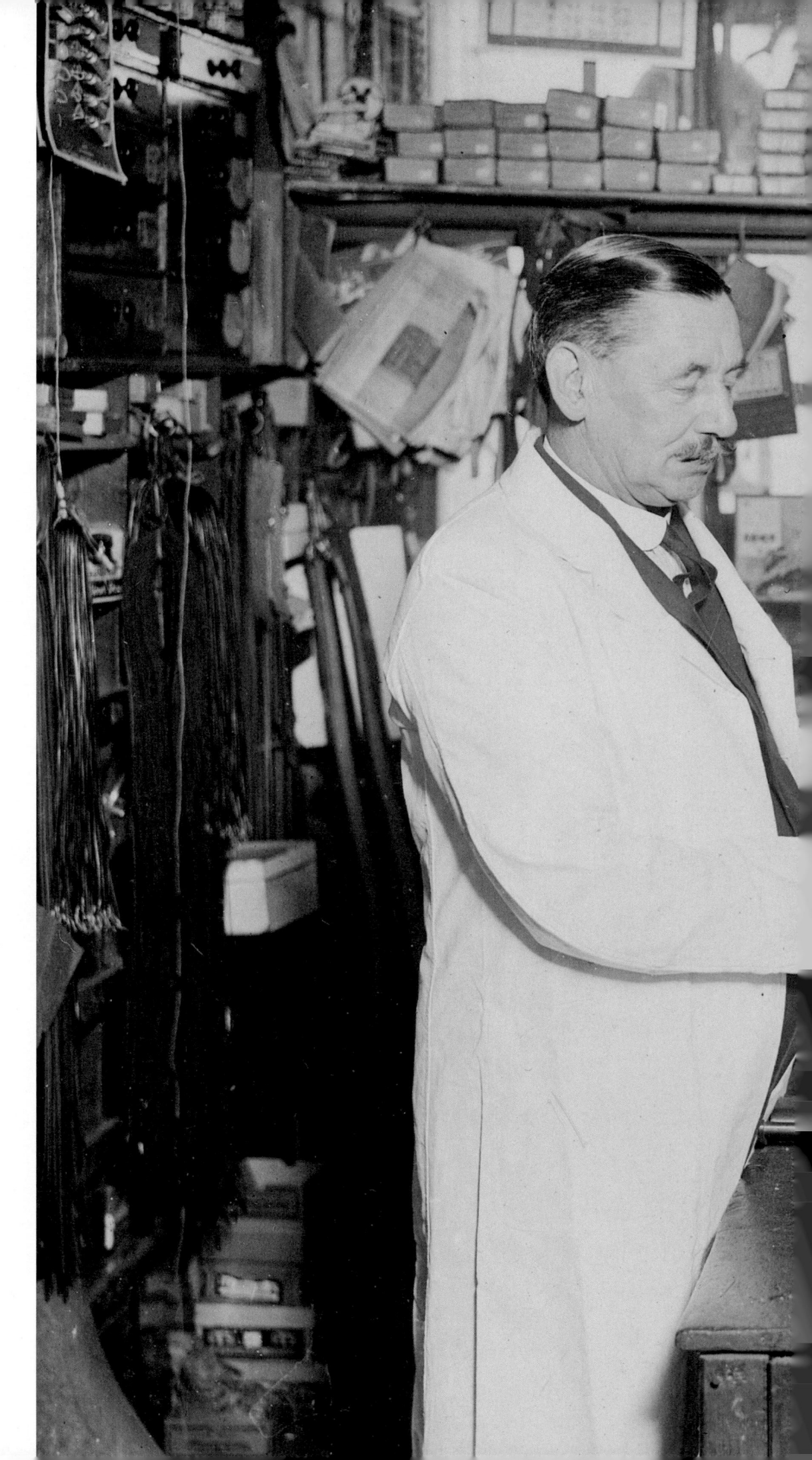

Preceding pages: Leytonstone after beating
local rivals Clapton Orient. May 1919.
Photograph by Nichols

Former Watford goalkeeper Bert Higgins
now owns a gentlemens' outfitters.
February 1932. Photograph by J.A. Hampton

Manchester City captain Roy Paul, with his son Ronald, leaves the pitch at Wembley after beating Birmingham City 3-1 in the FA Cup Final. May 1956. Photographer not known

Opposite: Birmingham City and Manchester City in the tunnel before kick-off. May 1956. Photographer not known

The coffin is a prop for a cowboy gunfight staged at The Den before Millwall's Sixth Round FA Cup tie against Ipswich Town. March 1978. Photographer not known

Opposite: Queens Park Rangers supporters before the League Cup Final against West Bromwich Albion. March 1967. Photographer not known

West Ham United's inside-forward Gordon Johnston, a promising light baritone, sings to his team-mates in the treatment room after training. November 1953.
Photographer not known

**Bolton Wanderers return home after beating
Manchester City 1–0 in the FA Cup Final. April 1926.**
Photographer not known

Bristol Rovers captain Ray Warren looks at the Eastville pitch, which is three feet under water, two days before the Third Round FA Cup tie against Aldershot, January 1951. Photograph by Burchell

Kick-off is delayed at White Hart Lane before the Third Round FA Cup replay between Tottenham Hotspur and Leeds United. January 1954. Photograph by Monty Fresco

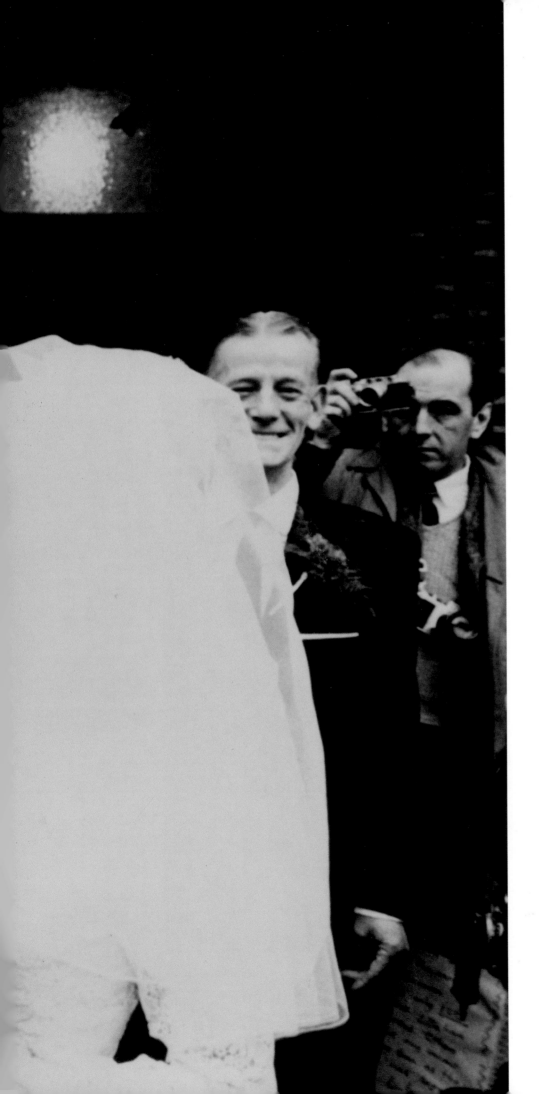

Chelsea's Terry Venables marries Christine McCann at
St Cedd's in Canning Town, London. Vicar Robin Bennett
is a West Ham United supporter. April 1966.
Photographer not known

Charlton Athletic supporters at The Valley. January 1938. Photograph by J.A. Hampton

Opposite: Aston Villa supporters before the FA Cup Final against Manchester United. May 1957. Photographer not known

Patients at Moorfields Eye Hospital, London, listen
to a radio broadcast of England versus Scotland.
The blackboard shows a grid, devised by the BBC,
that helps listeners fix the position of the ball
during play; it gave rise to the expression 'back to
square one'. April 1932. Photographer not known

Everton supporters, in London for the FA Cup Final, encounter Muhammad Ali, in training for his forthcoming fight against Henry Cooper. May 1966.
Photographer not known

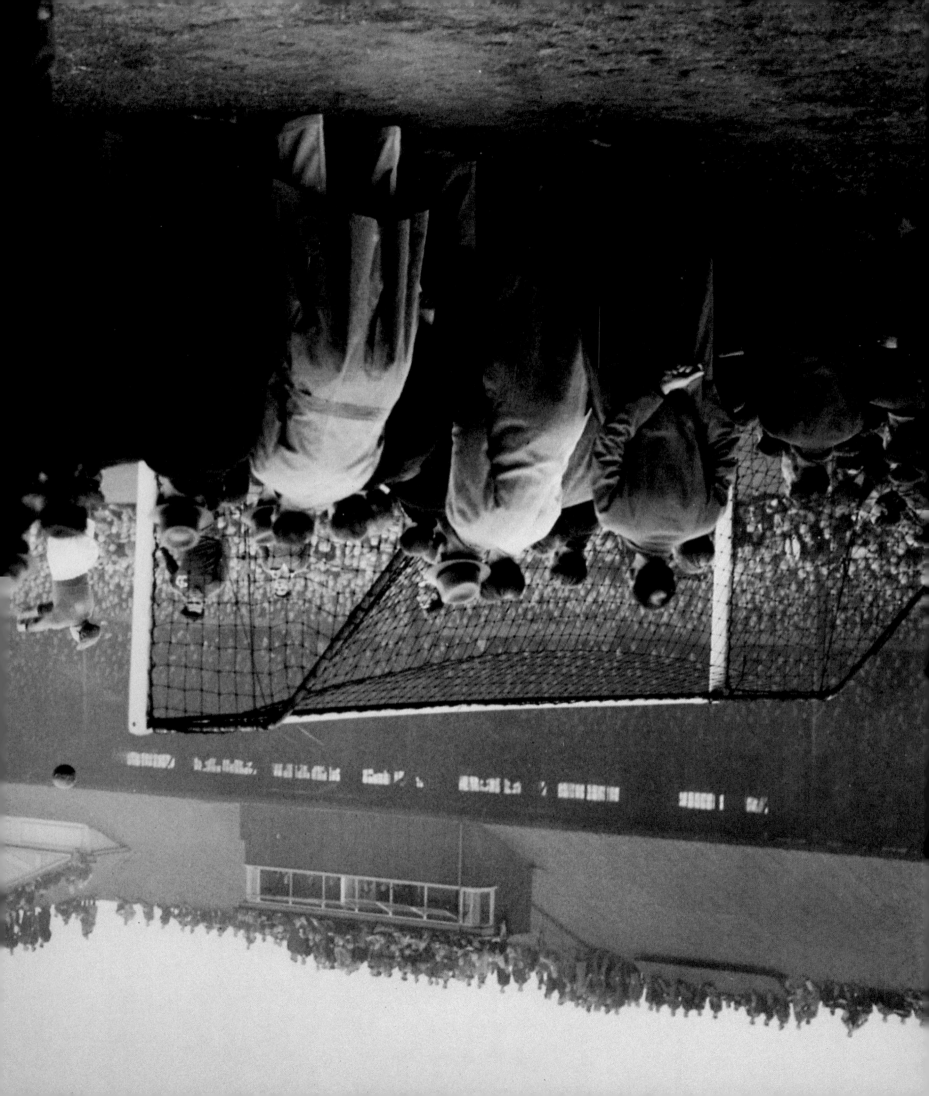

Stamford Bridge overflows
when Chelsea play a friendly
against Dynamo Moscow.
November 1945. Photographer
not known

301

Scotland supporters in Trafalgar Square, London, celebrating the 3–1
Home Championship defeat of England. April 1949. Photograph by J. Waldorf

Opposite: On the way to Wembley, where Scotland draw 1–1 with England.
April 1947. Photograph by John Drysdale

Portsmouth supporters, Fratton Park. December 1951. Photograph by George Douglas
Opposite: Sitting on barriers at The Den. January 1938. Photograph by E. Dean

Arsenal supporters at Kings Cross station on their way to Huddersfield for the FA Cup
Semi-final against Grimsby Town. March 1936. Photograph by E. Dean

Tottenham Hotspur supporters leave Euston station for the Fifth Round FA Cup tie against Everton. February 1937. Photograph by E. Dean

Mothers and babies queue
at the Town Hall for tickets
for Gateshead's Sixth Round
FA Cup tie against Bolton
Wanderers. February 1953.
Photograph by Lauder

Glasgow Rangers versus Celtic at Ibrox Park, October 1949. Photograph by John Chillingworth

Opposite: Police and players attempt to persuade a supporter to leave the pitch during Crystal Palace's Fourth Round FA Cup tie against Everton at Selhurst Park, January 1931. Photographer not known

A corner shop in Highbury, London. Bertie Mee's Arsenal have just won the First Division Championship by beating Tottenham Hotspur in the last game of the season. Days later they complete the double with a 2–1 win over Liverpool in the FA Cup Final. May 1971. Photographer not known

Opposite: Freida and Frank Hearn wait to board the 'Ipswich Special' taking Fulham supporters to their Second Round FA Cup tie. January 1957. Photograph by William Vanderson

Jimmy Greaves in AC Milan's San Siro stadium. Greaves started the 1961 season with AC but – after scoring nine times in 14 games – was playing for Tottenham Hotspur by December of the same year. April 1961. Photograph by Norman Quicke

Opposite: Missing an England training session to rest his shin, which was gashed in the World Cup group game against France. The injury keeps Greaves out of the team and, despite recovering, denies him a place in the Final against West Germany. July 1966. Photographer not known

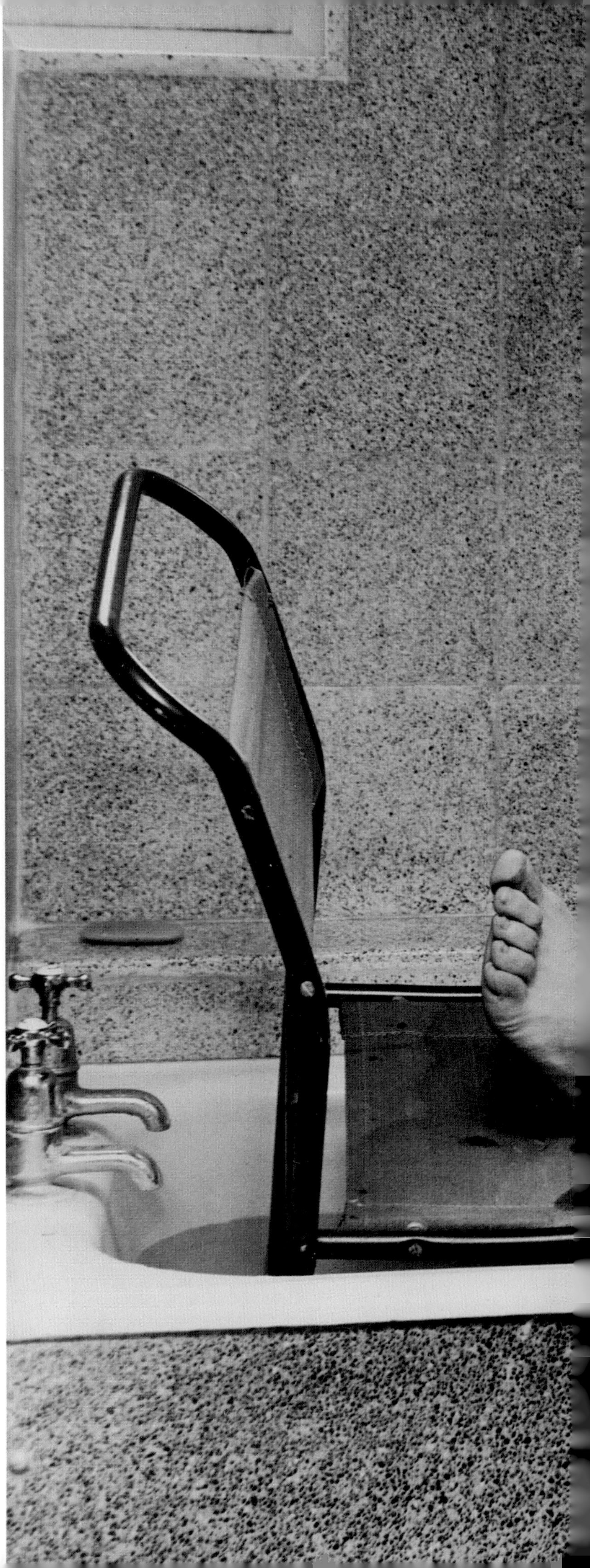

Miss Miller, football coach for Crawley Downs Church School, Surrey, with her squad. September 1931. Photographer not known

Miss Casey coaches the team, who were unbeaten last season, at her school in Bradford. September 1936. Photographer not known

Millwall captain Dave Magnall after his
team's 2–0 victory over Manchester City in
the Sixth Round of the FA Cup at The Den.
March 1937. Photographer not known

Millwall's lion mascot falls over as the team runs out. March 1927. Photograph by H.F. Davis

Opposite: The annual Jockeys versus Variety Artists charity game, to be held this year at Stamford Bridge, is postponed. December 1914. Photographer not known

Stanley Matthews signs autographs before his farewell game – a Stanley Matthews XI versus a World XI – at Stoke City's Victoria Ground. Alongside Matthews are Tony Waiters and Jimmy Armfield (Blackpool); George Cohen and Johnny Haynes (Fulham); Bobby Thompson (Wolverhampton Wanderers); Denis Law and Bobby Charlton (Manchester United); and Jimmy Greaves, Alan Gilzean and Cliff Jones (Tottenham Hotspur). Playing for the World XI are Lev Yashin (Russia); Karl Heinz Schnellinger and Wolfgang Weber (West Germany); Josef Masopust and Jan Popluhar (Czechoslovakia); Jim Baxter and Willie Henderson (Scotland); Raymond Kopa (France); Alfredo di Stefano (Spain); Ferenc Puskas (Hungary); and Eusebio (Portugal). April 1965. Photographer not known

Alf Ramsey with a crystal ball on which are engraved the names of England's World Cup-winning team. September 1966. Photograph by A. Jones

Opposite: At an England training session before a friendly against the USSR. February 1968. Photographer not known

St James's Park before
the FA Cup Quarter-final
against Hull City. March 1930.
Photographer not known

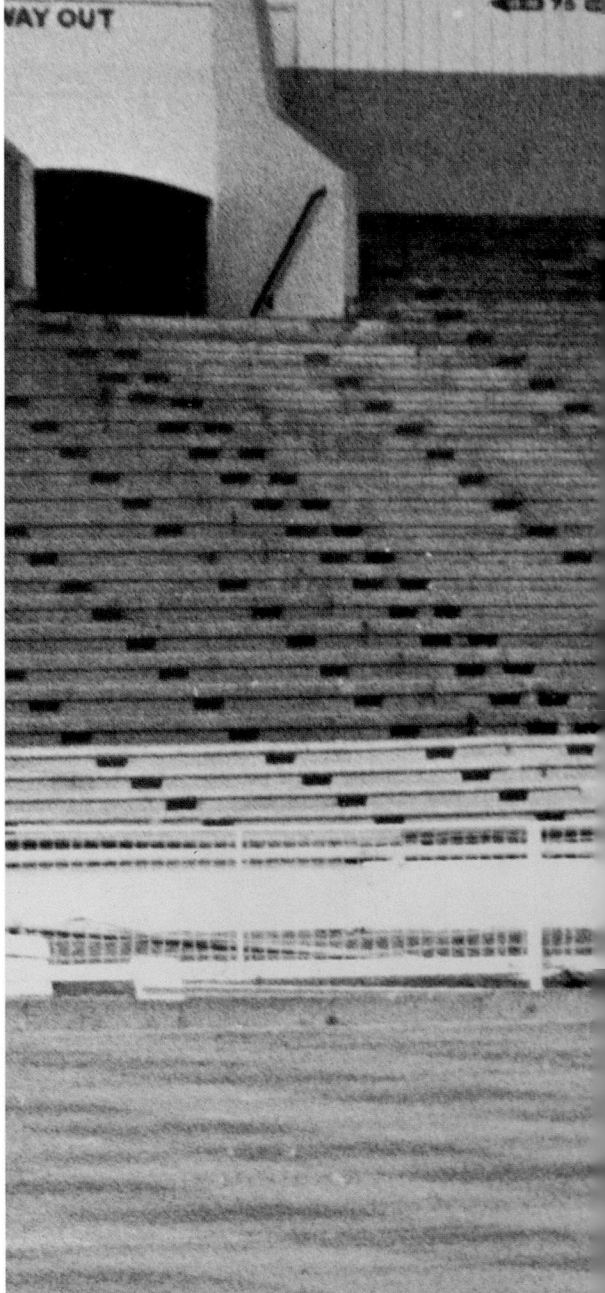

Nat Lofthouse leads Bolton Wanderers up to receive FA Cup winners' medals as the losing Manchester United manager, Matt Busby (in hat), walks away. May 1958. Photographer not known

Opposite: Busby tries out the Wembley pitch on the morning of the European Cup Final against Benfica. May 1968. Photographer not known

Street game, Brindley Road, Notting Hill, London. 1957. Photograph by Roger Mayne
Opposite: Street game, Southam Street, Notting Hill, London. 1956. Photograph by Roger Mayne

England Ladies versus France Ladies. May 1925. Photograph by Edward G. Malindine

Opposite: The Honourable Irene Lawley kicks off a Royal Army Medical Corps match. February 1916. Photographer not known

The wives and girlfriends of the Liverpool squad are in London for the FA Cup Final against Arsenal. May 1971. Photograph by Leonard Burt

Opposite: Ian St John travels back to Liverpool with the FA Cup after scoring the decisive goal in the 2–1 victory over Leeds United in the Final. May 1965. Photographer not known

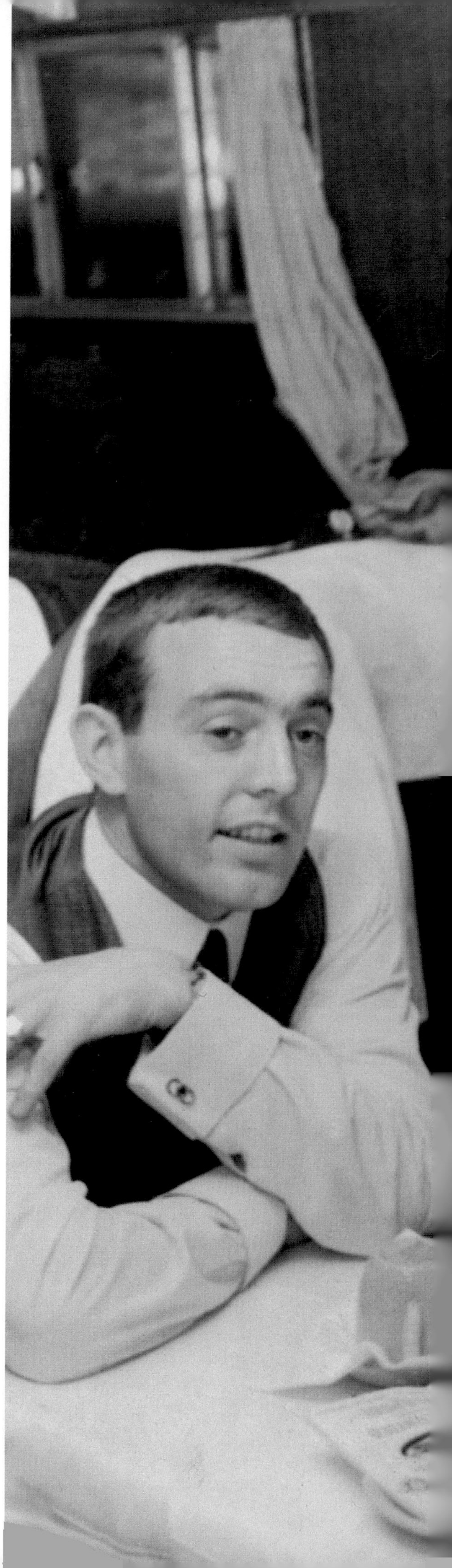

Newcastle United supporters before their Fifth Round FA Cup tie against Swansea City. February 1952. Photographer not known

Opposite: SS 'Bernicia' takes Newcastle United mascot 'Felix' to London for the FA Cup Final against Aston Villa. April 1924. Photograph by Brooke

Light is so bad in the second half of Charlton Athletic versus Burton Albion that spectators light newspapers to act as flares. January 1956. Photograph by Greaves

Opposite: A Blackpool supporter travels on the overnight 'Special' to London for the 1948 Cup Final against Manchester United. April 1948. Photographer not known

Following pages: Double-winning Tottenham Hotspur's pre-season photo-call at their training ground in Cheshunt, Hertfordshire. August 1961. Photographer not known

Plymouth Argyle trainer Tommy Haynes points the way to promotion, but next season finds them still in Division Three South. August 1926. Photograph by Gill

Opposite: Unidentified goalkeeper practises kicking. 1939. Photographer not known

Bobby and Tina Moore in matching cardigans for 'Woman's Realm'.
October 1965. Photographer not known

Opposite: Modelling for 'Vogue'. September 1962. Photograph by Peter Rand

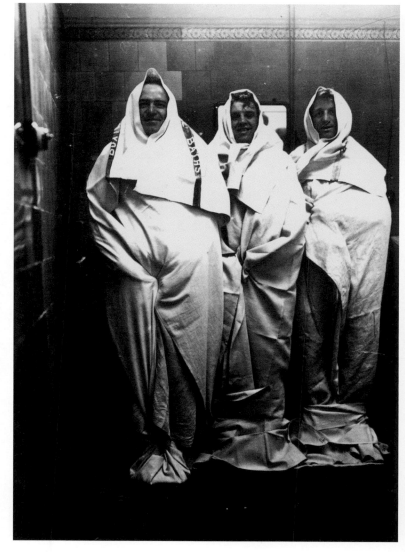

Left to right: right-back Jock Marshall, inside-forward
Jackie Carr and half-back Billy Ellerington of Middlesbrough.
1923. Photographer not known

Opposite: Sunlamp treatment at Highbury. January 1931.
Photographer not known

Jimmy Greaves signs autographs after making his Tottenham Hotspur debut in a reserve game at Plymouth Argyle. December 1961. Photographer not known

Tom Finney, the 'Preston Plumber', at work three months after his first-team debut for Preston North End. His father had advised him to get a trade. November 1946.
Photograph by Charles Hewitt

Opposite: Frank Cotterill, who played for Aston Villa, Southend United and Watford, has become a printer's reel-hand since retiring from the game. February 1932.
Photograph by J.A. Hampton

The England squad on the
day before the World Cup
Final. July 1966. Photograph
by Terry Fincher

Guards at the Tower of London. January 1929. Photographer not known

The Anfield boot-room. Left to right: Roy Evans, reserve team coach; Tom Saunders, European scout; Joe Fagan, assistant manager; Bob Paisley, manager; and Ronnie Moran, chief coach. May 1980. Photograph by John Dawes

Scotland supporters on the Strand, London. April 1947. Photographer not known

Opposite: The Metropolitan Police on duty during the World Cup Finals. July 1966. Photographer not known

JLITAN POLICE

INFORMATION
AND INTERPRETERS

RENSEICNEMENTS
LICE ET INTERPRETES

AUSKUNFTSSTELLE
POLIZEI UND DOLMETSCHER

INFORMAZIONE
E INTERPRETI

INFORMACION
POLIZIA E INTERPRETI

INFORMACION
E INTERPRETES

INFORMAÇÃO
E INTERPRETES

Manchester City supporters in Trafalgar Square before the FA Cup Final against Everton. April 1933. Photograph by J.A. Hampton

Opposite: An Everton supporter celebrates the 3–0 FA Cup Final victory over Manchester City in Trafalgar Square. April 1933. Photographer not known

Arsenal manager Tom Whittaker receives a painting, entitled 'Tom Whittaker's Secret', from a Mr A. Warwick of 'John Bull' magazine. On the right is the artist, Yates Wilson, who was originally commissioned by the magazine to paint a front cover. December 1947. Photographer not known

Opposite: The team recreate the scene at Highbury. From left to right: Ronnie Rooke, Leslie Compton, Archie MacAuly, James Logie, Wally Barnes, Reg Lewis, 'Paddy' Sloan, George Hale, Bryn Jones and Denis Compton. December 1947. Photographer not known

Autograph hunters at Highbury. August 1946. Photographer not known

Opposite: Supporters arrive at Wembley to see England versus Hungary. November 1953. Photographer not known

Bobby and Jackie Charlton in their home town of Ashington, Northumberland, after England's World Cup Final victory. August 1966. Photographer not known

Opposite: Bobby Charlton recovers in a Munich hospital after the aircrash that took the lives of eight of his team-mates. February 1958. Photographer not known

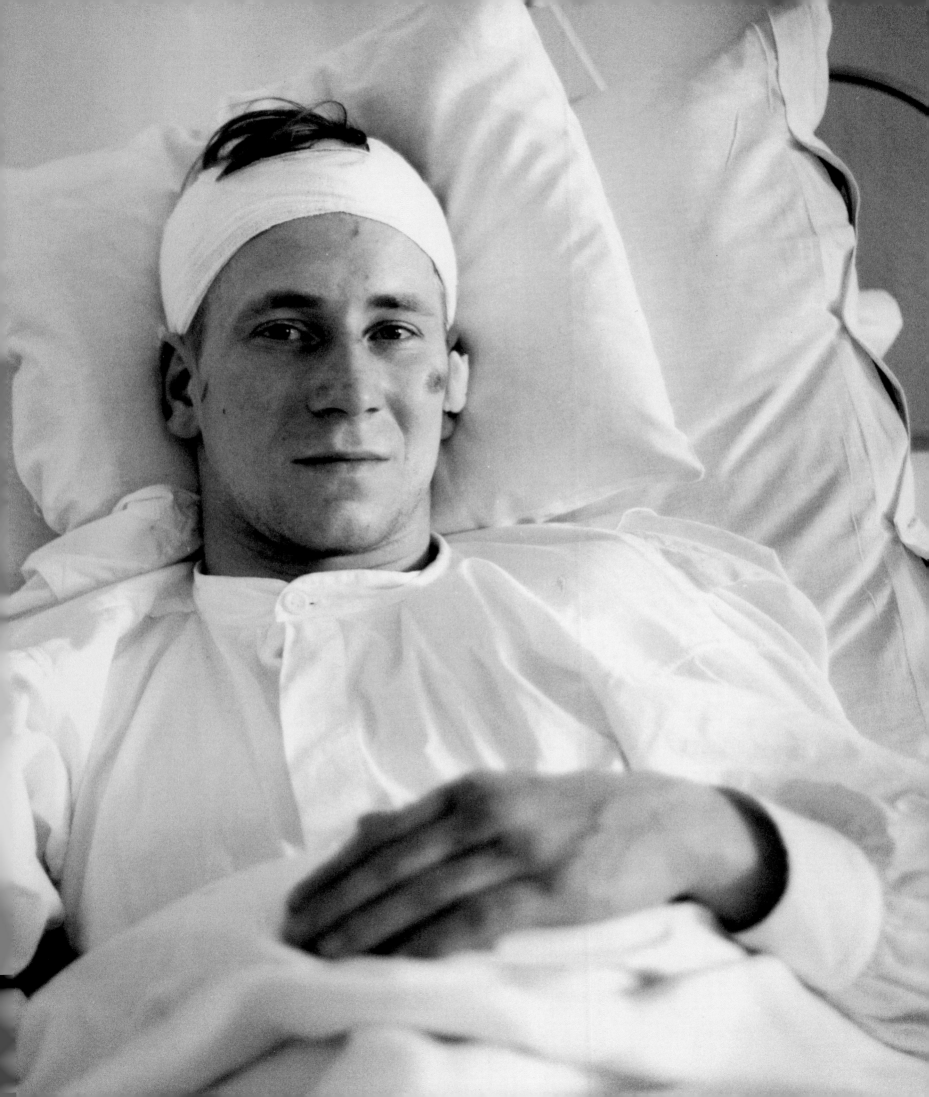

Arsenal versus Tottenham. The North Bank, Highbury.
January 1934. Photograph by A. Hudson

Back row, left to right: Phil Beal, Tottenham Hotspur; Martin Buchan, Manchester United; Malcolm Allison, Manchester City manager; Martin Chivers, Tottenham Hotspur; Gordon Banks, Stoke City; Terry Mancini, Queens Park Rangers. Front row, left to right: Rodney Marsh, Manchester City; Francis Lee, Manchester City; Dave Webb, Chelsea; Geoff Hurst, Stoke City. Allison, 'The Godfather', and his capos meet in a Manchester restaurant. September 1972. Photograph by Terry O'Neill

Opposite: back row, left to right: Alan Ball, Arsenal; Geoff Hurst, West Ham United; Terry Venables, Queens Park Rangers. Front row, left to right: Terry Mancini, Queens Park Rangers; Dave Webb, Chelsea; Alan Hudson, Chelsea; Rodney Marsh, Queens Park Rangers. They call themselves 'The Clan' and are pictured here at Trattoria Est on London's Fleet Street. March 1972. Photograph by Terry O'Neill

West Bromwich Albion at Paddington station
after beating Birmingham City 2–1 in the FA Cup Final.
April 1931. Photographer not known

Bill Shankly answers fan mail at home in Liverpool. October 1975.
Photograph by John Dawes

Opposite: Following Liverpool's 2–1 defeat of Leeds United in the
FA Cup Final. May 1965. Photograph by Michael Webb

George Best outside Mrs Fullaway's – his digs in Manchester.
1965. Photograph by Ray Green

Opposite: At Manchester United's Cliff training ground in Salford.
1964. Photographer not known

Goalkeeper Jim Sanders looks away as team-mate Ronnie Allen equalises from the penalty spot for West Bromwich Albion in the FA Cup Final against Preston North End. Albion go on to win 3–2. May 1954.
Photographer not known

INDEX

A

AC Milan 314
Adams, Ilona 173
aerial views
  Hackney Marshes 164-165
  Wembley 1930 Cup Final 34-35
Aldwych Theatre 168-169
Allan, Ernie 265
Allen, Ronnie 378-379
Allison, Malcolm 370
Anfield see Liverpool
Anstey's Cove beach 72-73
Argentina v. England 1966
  130-131
Arsenal
  1926 snow, v. Manchester
    United 160-161
  1929 Charity Cup celebrity
    kick-off 60-61
  1930 Clock End 56-57
  1930 FA Cup parade 242-243
  1931 sunlamp treatment 346-347
  1934 ice bath 166
  1934 spectators 368-369
  1936 supporters 75, 306
  1938 dressing room 94-95
  1940s team in military uniforms 218
  1945 ticket queues for game v.
    Dynamo Moscow 224-225
  1946 autograph hunters 364
  1947 laundry 223
  1947 'Tom Whittaker's Secret'
    (painting) 362-363
  1950 training 156
  1951 spectators 176-177
  1951 supporters 190-191
  1962 training 96-97
  1971 supporter's shop 313
  Baker, Joe 42-43
  Ball, Alan 370-371
  Barnes, Wally 362-363
  Bastin, Cliff 194-195
  Compton, Denis 362-363
  Compton, Leslie 362-363
  Copping, Wilf 166
  Drake, Ted 128
  Eastham, George 42-43
  Hale, George 362-363
  Jones, Bryn 362-363
  Lewis, Reg 362-363
  Logie, James 362-363
  MacAuly, Archie 362-363
  Rooke, Ronnie 362-363
  Sloan, 'Paddy' 362-363
  Whittaker, Tom 362
Ashbourne shrovetide village
  game 14-15, 270, 271
Ashington, World Cup parade 366
Aston Villa
  1958 FA Cup Final supporters 295
  Cotterill, Frank 350-351
Atherstone street football
  game 256-257
autograph hunters
  1946 Arsenal 364
  1961 Jimmy Greaves 348-349
automated crossing machine 18
Ayresome Park see Middlesborough

B

'back to square one' 296-297
Baker, Joe 42-43
Ball, Alan 42-43, 370-371
ball manufacturers, Webbers 29
ball, plastic 152-153
ball-propelling machine 156
ball selection, World Cup 1966 28
ballet training 216-217
Banks, Gordon 42-43, 370
Barnes, Wally 362-363
Barnett, Laurie 247
Barnsley
  1910 mascot 231
  1961 supporters 22
Bastin, Cliff 194-195
beach scenes
  Leigh-on-Sea mud football
    1925: 192-193
  Stanley Matthews on Blackpool
    beach 1953: 16-17
  Torquay United at Anstey's
    Cove 1938: 72-73
Beal, Phil 370
Bennett, Revd Robin 292-293
'Bernicia', SS 336-337
Best, George 90-91, 376, 377
Beverley School, New Malden 139
Beverley Sisters, The 238
Bingham, Billy 38-39
Birmingham City
  1956 FA Cup Final 282
  1965 training 157
  Lynn, Stan 157
Blackburn Rovers
  Marshall, Jack 204-205
  Newton, Keith 42-43
Blackheath 162-163
Blackmore, Harry 186
Blackpool
  1936 silence for death of HM
    King George V 117
  1948 supporters 253, 338
  Ball, Alan 42-43
  Stuart, Ronnie 204-205
Blackpool beach 16-17
Blanchflower, Richard 200-201
Blenheim Palace 178
Bolton Wanderers
  1926 FA Cup Final trip 82-83
  1926 FA Cup parade 288-289
  1958 FA Cup Final 142, 328
  Blackmore, Harry 186
  Lofthouse, Nat 184-185, 187, 328
  Pym, Dick 186
  Ridding, Bill 187
  Seddon, Jimmy 186
Bonetti, Peter 146-147
boots
  1936 Charlton Athletic
    boot-rooom 222
  1938 Ted Drake 128
  1952 Portsmouth kit 104-105
  1980 Liverpool boot-room 356-357
  Nigerian support straps 120-121
  special kicking pad 129
  Tornado design 129
box office staff, Wembley
  Stadium 109
Bradford schoolboys 317
Bremner, Billy 106-107, 208-209
Brentford, manager commentates
  for blind supporters 144-145
Brighton and Hove Albion 172
brine bath 135
Bristol Rovers
  1951 flood 290
  1958 supporters 150
  Warren, Ray 290

British Army XI 52-53
British Industries Fair 1955: 249
broadcast commentaries, square
  system 296-297
Brough, R.H. 118-119
Brown, Alan 204-205
Brown, Ken 260-261
Buchan, Martin 370
Buckingham Palace 179
Burkett, Jack 12-13
Burnley
  Harris, Gordon 42-43
  Potts, Harry 204-205
Burr, Yvonne 216-217
Busby, Matt 204-205, 219, 328-329
Buxton Town 76

C

Carr, Jackie 347
cake for Southampton 50th
  anniversary 263
Cannes 124-125
card game 168-169
Cardiff City
  1921 spectators 126-127
  Davis, Len 147
Carey, John 204-205
Carrow Road see Norwich City
Casey, Miss 317
Catterick, Harry 204-205
celebrity kick-offs
  1916 Lawley, Hon Irene 332-333
  1916 Royal Army Medical Corps
    match 1916: 332-333
  1921 Sandhurst, HRH Prince
    of Wales 60
  1929 Charity Cup Final 60-61
Central Hall 265
Charity Cup 1929, celebrity
  kick-off 60-61
Charity Shield 1974 208-209
Charlton Athletic
  1934 terracing construction
    154-155
  1938 supporters 294
  1956 flares needed v. Burton
    Albion 339
  Welsh, Don 219
Charlton, Bobby 42-43, 366-367
Charlton, Jack 42-43, 106-107,
  209, 366
Charlton, Mrs Cissie 248-249
Chelsea
  1914 walking noticeboard 320
  1932 training 64
  1939 restaurant support 30-31
  1939 treatment 77
  1941 wartime international 52-53
  1945 v. Dynamo Moscow 300-301
  1949 programme seller 210
  1963 Cannes holiday 124-125
  1963 tactics training 240
  1966 goalkeepers 146-147
  Bonetti, Peter 146-147
  Hudson, Alan 370-371
  Medhurst, Harry 139
  Sexton, Dave 240, 261
  Stepney, Alex 146-147
  Venables, Terry 180-181, 292-293
  Webb, Dave 370, 370-371
Chisholm, Kenneth 38-39
Chivers, Martin 370
cinema newsreel, 1964 FA Cup Final
  in Cinemascope 236-237

Clan, The 370-371
Clydebank shipyard 170-171
coaching during game 86-87
cockerel cleaning 189
cod (mascot) 202-203
coffin prop 285
Cohen, George 42-43, 130-131
Colchester United
  1950 supporters club hut 103
  1950 v. Norwich City 102
Colley, Mrs 239
Compton, Denis 362-363
Compton, Leslie 362-363
Cooper, Tommy 173
Copping, Wilf 166
Craven Cottage see Fulham
Crawley Downs Church
  School 316
Crazy Gang, The 100-101
crowd control 68-69
Crownshaw, Ray 262
Crystal Palace
  1914 spectators 148-149
  1931 spectator on the pitch 311
'Cuckoo in the Nest' (play) 168-169

D

Dagenham, Banham Road 260-261
Daniel, Ray 38-39
Davis, Len 147
deaf and dumb teams
  England v. Wales 1925 161
Den, The see Milwall
donkey (mascot) 231
shower massage treatment 76
Drake, Ted 128
dressing room, Arsenal 1938 94-95
Dynamo Moscow
  1945 ticket queue for game v.
    Arsenal 224-225
  1945 v. Chelsea 300-301

E

East Kent Packers 84
Eastham, George 42-43
Eastville see Bristol Rovers
Ebenezer 121
Edward VIII, HM King 60
Electronic Summation System 78
Elizabeth II, HM Queen 249
Elland Road see Leeds United
Ellerington, Billy 347
Elliott, Billy 38-39
Embankment, London 20-21
England
  1925 deaf and dumb match v.
    Wales 161
  1953 supporters 365
  1966 squad in club colours 42-43
  1966 v. Argentina 130-131
Epping Forest 212-213
European Cup
  1968 Final 328-329
  1968 Final spectator 214
  the cup itself 254-255
Euston station 248-249, 266-267
Evans, Roy 356-357
Evans, Spencer 247
Everton
  1927 supporters 266-267
  1933 supporter FA Cup Final 360
  1966 FA Cup Final 196-197
  1966 FA Cup Final supporters
    298-299

1968 supporters 151
Catterick, Harry 204-205
Mercer, Joe 219
Temple, Derek 196-197
Wilson, Ray 42-43

F
FA Cup – matches other than Finals
  1923 Plymouth Argyle 174-175
  1933 West Ham United
    supporters 88-89
  1938 Ipswich Town 48-49
  1961 Barnsley supporters 22
  1967 draw for third round 118-119
FA Cup Finals
  1923 flagpole 132
  1923 West Ham United
    supporters 66-67
  1924 Newcastle United mascot
    Felix 336-337
  1926 Bolton Wanderes 82-83
  1929 Bolton Wanderers 186
  1930 Graf Zeppelin 34-35
  1931 West Bromwich Albion 372-373
  1933 Everton supporter 360
  1933 Manchester City
    supporters 361
  1934 Manchester City
    celebration 232-233
  1935 cameraman 159
  1936 crowd control 68-69
  1936 Sheffield United
    supporters 122-123
  1948 Blackpool supporter 338
  1950 television viewing 26-27
  1954 West Bromwich Albion v.
    Preston North End 378-37
  1956 Birmingham City v.
    Manchester City 282
  1958 Aston Villa supporters 295
  1958 Bolton Wanderers 187
  1958 Bolton Wanderers v.
    Manchester United 328
  1959 Luton Town supporters 273
  1962 Tottenham Hotspur 200-201
  1963 Manchester United 226
  1963 ticket allocation protest 108
  1965 Liverpool, Bill Shankly 374-375
  1966 Everton 196-197
  1968 Paul McCartney 274
  1971 Liverpool wives and ladies 334
  1973 Sunderland 196
  1974 locked out supporters 215
FA Cup – the Cup itself 118, 136, 137,
  186, 187, 200-201, 220-221, 232-233,
  236-237, 334-335, 340-341
FA Cup parades
  1921 Tottenham Hostspur 136
  1926 Bolton Wanderers 288-289
  1930 Arsenal 242-243
  1950 Wolverhampton Wanderers
    220-221
  1959 Nottingham Forest 142-143
  1962 Tottenham Hotspur 200-201
FIFA, Sir Stanley Rous 28
factory workers 36-37
Fagan, Joe 254-255, 356-357
Fairbrother, Jack 105
fashion photographs 344-345
Felix (mascot) 336-337
filming
  1935 FA Cup Final cameraman 159
  1935 schoolboys 158-159
  1949 Leicester City matches 83

Finney, Tom 350
flares, 1956 Charlton Athletic v.
  Burton Albion 339
floods
  1926 Essex 206-207
  1951 Bristol Rovers 290
  1954 Tottenham Hotspur 291
Flowers, Ron 42-43
flu prevention 1933: 32
Football League Championship
  trophy 71, 340-341
Forsyth, Bruce 140
Fraser, Ian 262
Fratton Park see Portsmouth
frost
  1925 Tottenham Hostspur 115
  1938 Stoke City 114-115
Fulham
  1936 silence for death of HM
    King George V 117
  1957 supporters 312
  1958 ticket tout 40-41
  1963 silence for death of
    President J.F. Kennedy 116
  Cohen, George 42-43

G
Garnett, Alf (Warren Mitchell) 92
Gateshead 308-309
Germany
  1935 Nazi salute 259
  1935 v. England 259
Gibbons, Jackie 144-145
Glasgow Rangers, Willie Wadell 250
goalkeeper (unidentified) 343
Goldie (golden eagle) 80-81
Graf Zeppelin 34-35
Greaves, Jimmy 42-43, 110,
  314-315, 348-349
Greenhaigh, Jim 246
Greenwood, Ron 236-237
Grimsby Town 202-203
Grimsdell, Arthur 136

H
Hackney Marshes from the
  air 164-165
Hale, George 362-363
Hampden Park ground, Rod
  Stewart 1974: 275
Hardy Amies suit, worn by
  Bobby Moore 55
Harmer, Englebert K 129
Harris, Gordon 42-43
Harris, Johnny 204-205
Harrow school 272
Haynes, Tommy 342
Hearn, Frank 312
Hearn, Freda 312
heat-treatment 12-13
Hibernian, Ally McLeod 251
Higgins, Bert 280-281
Highbury see Arsenal
Hornsey YMCA 163
Houghton, Frank 105
Hudson, Alan 370-371
Hull City
  Greenhaigh, Jim 246
  Hunter, Norman 42-43
  Hurst, Geoff 42-43, 370, 370-371

I
ice bath 166
ice, 1963 Leeds United 209

Ipswich Town 48-49
Islington Town Hall 242-243

J
'John Bull' (magazine) painting 362
Johnston, Gordon 286-287
Jones, Bryn 362-363

K
Keegan, Kevin 208-209
Kensington Town Hall 26-27
Kerr, Bobby 196
kickabouts
  1931 Royal Albert Docks 170
  1933 London school 113
  1950 London street 228-229
  1955 Salford schoolboys 112
  1956 Southam Street, Notting
    Hill 331
  1957 Brindley Road, Notting Hill 330
  1962 London street 99
  1967 Clydebank shipyard 170-171
  1969 Purley Way 73
Kilmarnock factory workers 36-37

L
ladies' football
  1925 England Ladies v. France
    Ladies 333
  1953 East Kent Packers 84
  1953 Maldon Ladies FC 85
  Chittenden, Brenda 84
  Law, Denis 226-227
League Cup Final 1967 284-285
Lee, Francis 370
Leeds United
  1950s Electronic Summation
    System 78
  1963 ice 209
  Bremner, Billy 106-107
  Charlton, Jack 42-43, 106-107, 209
  Hunter, Norman 42-43
  Reaney, Paul 42-43
  Revie, Don 204-205
Leicester City
  1949 filming matches 83
  1949 team lunch 241
  Banks, Gordon 42-43
Leigh-on-Sea 192-193
Lewis, Reg 362-363
Leytonstone F C 278-279
lion mascot 321
Littlehampton Boys' Club 216-217
Littlewoods pools winners
  44-45, 140-141
Liverpool
  1965 FA Cup Final 334-335
  1971 FA Cup Final wives and
    ladies 334
  1983 League championship
    trophy 71
  1984 European Cup 254-255
  Busby, Matt 219
  Evans, Roy 356-357
  Fagan, Joe 254-255, 356-357
  Milne, Gordon 42-43
  Moran, Ronnie 356-357
  Paisley, Bob 70, 71, 356-357
  Saunders, Tom 356-357
  Shankly, Bill 374-375
  Smith, Tommy 24
  St John, Ian 334-335
  Stevenson, Willie 42-43
  Thompson, Peter 42-43

Lofthouse, Nat 184-185, 187, 328
Logie, James 362-363
Luton Town
  supporters 1959 273
Lynn, Stan 157

M
MacAuly, Archie 362-363
MacDowall, Les 204-205
Magnall, Dave 318-319
Maine Road see Manchester City
Maldon Ladies FC 85
Mall, The 122-123
maltec milk 33
Manchester City
  1926 supporters 252-253
  1933 FA Cup Final supporters 361
  1934 FA Cup celebration 232-233
  1956 FA Cup Final 282, 283
  Allison, Malcolm 370
  Barnett, Laurie 247
  Evans, Spencer 247
  Lee, Francis 370
  Marsh, Rodney 370
  Poyser, George 204-205
  Revie, Don 244-245
  Roy, Paul 293
  Swift, Frank 62-63
  Walsh, Eilly 247
Manchester United
  1926 snow v. Arsenal 160-161
  1958 FA Cup Final 328
  1958 Munich crash 234-235, 366-367
  1968 European Cup Final 328-329
  1968 supporter 214
  Best, George 90-91, 376, 377
  Busby, Matt 204-205, 328-329
  Buchan, Martin 370
  Charlton, Bobby 42-43, 366-367
  Law, Denis 227
  Rowley, Jack 134-135
  Stiles, Nobby 24-25, 42-43
Mancini, Terry 370, 370-371
Mannion, Wilf 245
Marsh, Rodney 370, 370-371
Marshall, Jack 204-205
Marshall, Jock 347
mascots
  cod (Grimsby Town 1939) 202-203
  donkey (Barnsley 1910) 231
  Felix (Newcastle United 1924)
    336-337
  lion (Millwall 1927) 321
Matthews, Stanley 16-17, 114-115,
  322-323
McCann, Christine 292-293
McCartney, Paul 274
McLaren, Jim 19
McLeod, Ally 251
Medhurst, Harry 139
Mercer, Joe 219
Middlesborough
  1923 treatment 347
  1951 pensioner supporters 199
  Carr, Jackie 347
  Ellerington, Billy 347
  Mannion, Wilf 245
  Marshall, Jock 347
  Miller, Miss 316
Millwall
  1927 lion mascot 321
  1936 The Crazy Gang 100-101
  1937 supporters 318-319
  1937 v. Manchester City 318-319

1938 spectators 305
1978 coffin prop 285
 Magnall, Dave 318-319
Milne, Gordon 42-43
Milne, Jimmy 204-205
Mitchell, Warren 92
Molyneux see Wolverhampton
 Wanderers
Moore, Bobby 42-43, 54, 55,
 212-213, 344-345
Moore, Mrs Tina 212-213, 345
Moorfields Eye Hospital 296-297
Moran, Ronnie 356-357
mud football 192-193
Muhammad Ali 298-299
Munich aircrash 234-235, 366-367

N

National Stamp Exhibition 1966: 265
Neil, Billy 138
Newcastle United
 1924 mascot Felix 336-337
 1930 St James's Park 326-327
 1952 supporters 337
 Fairbrother, Jack 105
 Houghton, Frank 105
newspaper sellers 20-21
Newton, Keith 42-43
Nicholson, Keith 140
Nicholson, Mrs Viv 140-141
Nigeria
 Ebenezer 121
 support straps, not boots 120-121
Norwich City
 1950 spectators 198
 1950 v. Colchester United 102
Notting Hill 330, 331
Nottingham Forest
 1959 FA Cup parade 142-143
 Carey, John 204-205
Notts County
 1923 supporter 230
 Plackett, Sidney 110-111

O

O'Harte, Johnny 77
Old Trafford see Manchester United
Oldham Athletic, Les MacDowall
 204-205

P

Packham, Fred 118
Paisley, Bob 70, 71, 356-357
Paul, Ronald 283
Peterborough United theatre
 trip 1955 173
Peters, Ronald 216-217
Pickles (dog) 264-265
Pilkington, Roy 142
Plackett, Sidney 110-111
players working outside football
 gentleman's outfitters 280-281
 plumber 350
 printers reel-hand 350-351
 public relations officer 62-63
Plymouth Argyle
 1922 supporters 74
 1923 supporters and balloon 174-175
 1926 team training 342
 1950 FA Cup 3rd round tie 220-221
 Haynes, Tommy 342
police
 1931 spectator on pitch, Crystal
 Palace v. Everton 311

1937 clearing way for Milwall
 player 318-319
1947 Scotland supporters 358
1949 spectator, Rangers v.
 Celtic 310
1962 rush for tickets 268-269
1966 World Cup duty 359
1978 guarding mock coffin,
 Millwall 285
1984 guarding European Cup 254-255
pools winners 44-45, 140-141
Porteous, Trevor 204-205
Portsmouth
 1934 supporter 51
 1951 supporter 304
 Wright, Bill 104-105
Potts, Harry 204-205
Poyser, George 204-205
prams and ticket queue 308-309
precarious viewing
 1914 Crystal Palace 148-149
 1921 Cardiff City 126-127
 1938 Millwall 305
 1950 Norwich 198
Preston North End
 1954 FA Cup Final 378-379
 Finney, Tom 350
 Milne, Jimmy 204-205
Prince of Wales theatre 173
programme seller 210
Purdon, Ted 38-39
Purley Way 73
Pym, Dick 186

Q

QE2 (ship) 170-171
Queens Park Rangers
 1967 supporters 284-285
 Mancini, Terry 370, 370-371
 Marsh, Rodney 370-371
 Venables, Terry 370-371

R

Ramsay, Alf 130-131, 204-205,
 324, 325
rattles 50-51
Reaney, Paul 42-43
Remote Control Telesonic
 Apparatus 86-87
restaurant support for
 Chelsea 30-31
results in newspapers 20-21
Revie, Don 204-205, 244-245
Ridding, Bill 187
Rimet, Jules 369
Roberts, John 262
Robinson, Ike 204-205
Rooke, Ronnie 362-363
Rous, Sir Stanley 28
Rowley, Jack 134-135
Roy, Paul 283
Royal Albert Docks 170
Russell, Dave 204-205

S

San Siro stadium 314
Sanders, Jim 378-379
Sandhurst 60
Saudi Arabia stadium design 262
Saunders, Tom 356-357
schoolboys
 1931 Crawley Downs Church
 School 316
 1931 Walthamstow Schoolboys 98

1933 kickabout, London 113
1935 filming 158-159
1936 Bradford 317
1947 Billy Neil, emigrating 138
1948 St Joseph's College 58-59
1949 Beverley School, New
 Malden 139
1955 kickabout, Salford 112
1955 Littlehampton Boy's Club
 ballet training 216-217
1955 Manchester 244-245
1957 Saint Joseph's Academy
 162-163
1965 Banham Road, Dagenham
 260-261
Scotland
 1947 supporter 302-303
 1948 supporters 358
 1949 supporters 303
 1967 supporter 227
 1974 Rod Stewart 275
Seddon, Jimmy 186
Selhurst Park see Crytal Palace
Sexton, Dave 240, 261
Shankly, Bill 374-375
Sheffield United
 1936 supporters 122-123
 Harris, Johnny 204-205
Sheffield Wednesday
 1940s supporters 10-11
 Brown, Alan 204-205
 Springett, Ron 42-43
Shepherdson, Harold 42-43
Shrovetide game 14-15
silence
 1936 death of HM King George V 117
 1963 death of President J F
 Kennedy 116
Sims, Nigel 167
Sloan, 'Paddy' 362-363
Smith, George 58-59
Smith, Jacky 77
Smith, Norman 77
Smith, Stephen 200-201
Smith, Tommy 24
snow
 1926 Arsenal v. Manchester
 United 160-161
 1929 Tower of London 354-355
 1965 Fulham spectators 46-47
 1968 Alf Ramsey 325
Southampton 1935 50th anniversary
 cake 263
Southend United, Frank Cotterill
 350-351
special kicking pad 129
spectators
 1914 Crystal Palace 148-149
 1921 Cardiff City 126-127
 1930 West Ham United 182-183
 1934 Arsenal 368-369
 1938 Millwall 305
 1941 wartime international 52-53
 1949 Rangers v. Celtic 310
 1950 Norwich City 198
 1951 Brentford 144-145
 1951 Arsenal 176-177
 1965 Fulham in the snow 46-47
 1968 West Ham United 92
 and see supporters
Springett, Ron 42-43
St James's Park see Newcastle
 United
St John, Ian 334-335

St Joseph's Academy 162-163
St Joseph's College 58-59
stadia construction
 1923 Wembley 132-133
 1930 Highbury, Arsenal 56-57
 1934 The Valley, Charlton Athletic
 154-155
 1934 White Hart Lane, Tottenham
 Hotspur 188-189
 1936 White Hart Lane, Tottenham
 Hotspur 56
Stamford Bridge see Chelsea
Stampex 1966: 265
Stanley Gibbons 265
Stepney, Alex 146-147
Stevenson, Willie 42-43
Stewart, Rod 275, 276-277
Stiles, Nobby 24-25, 42-43
Stockport County, Trevor
 Porteous 204-205
Stoke City
 1938, braziers and frost 114-115
 Banks, Gordon 370
 Hurst, Geoff 370
 Matthews, Stanley 114-115, 322-323
Stokoe, Bob 196
Strand 358
Stuart, Ronnie 204-205
Sunderland
 1954 practice in the snow 38-39
 1973 FA Cup Final 196
 Bingham, Billy 38-39
 Chisholm, Kenneth 38-39
 Daniel, Ray 38-39
 Elliott, William 38-39
 Kerr, Bobby 196
 Purdon, Ted 38-39
 Stokoe, Bob 196
 Wright, Tom 38-39
supporters
 1922 Plymouth Argyle 74
 1923 Notts County 230
 1923 Plymouth Argyle 174-175
 1923 West Ham United, FA Cup
 Final 66-67
 1926 'Ye Silent Twins' 252-253
 1926 Manchester City 252-253
 1927 Everton 266-267
 1933 Everton FA Cup Final 360
 1933 Manchester City FA Cup
 Final 361
 1934 Portsmouth 51
 1935 West Bromwich Albion 50-51
 1936 Arsenal 75
 1936 Arsenal 306
 1936 Sheffield United 122-123
 1937 Millwall 318-319
 1937 Tottenham Hotspur 307
 1938 Charlton Athletic 294
 1940s Sheffield Wednesday 10-11
 1947 Scotland 302-303
 1948 Blackpool 253
 1948 Blackpool 338
 1948 Scotland 358
 1949 Scotland 303
 1949 Wolverhampton Wanderers 93
 1949 Wolverhampton Wanderers 211
 1949 Yeovil Town FA Cup 23
 1950 Colchester United club hut 103
 1951 Arsenal 190-191
 1951 Middlesborough 199
 1951 Portsmouth 304
 1952 Newcastle United 337
 1953 England v. Hungary 365

1957 Fulham 312
1958 Aston Villa FA Cup Final 295
1958 Bristol Rovers 150
1959 Luton Town 273
1961 Barnsley 22
1966 Everton FA Cup Final 298-299
1967 Queens Park Rangers 284-285
1967 Scotland 227
1968 Everton 151
1968 Manchester United 214
1968 West Ham United reverend 292-293
1971 Arsenal supporter's shop 313
1975 boots removed 40
and see spectators
supporters, locked out
1949 Wolverhampton Wanderers 211
1968 Wembley European Cup Final 214
1974 Wembley FA Cup Final 215
Swift, Frank 62-63

T
television, FA Cup Final 1950 26-27
Temple, Derek 196-197
Thompson, Peter 42-43
tickets
1945 Arsenal v. Dynamo Moscow queues 224-225
1945 Wembley Stadium box office staff 109
1953 Gateshead queue and prams 308-309
1958 Craven Cottage tout 40-41
1962 White Hart Lane rush 268-269
1963 FA Cup Final allocation protest 108
Tornado boot design 129
Torquay United, beach practice 1938: 72-73
Tottenham Hotspur
1921 FA Cup parade 136
1923 as 'beavers' 258
1925 straw and frost 115
1933 flu prevention 32
1934 cockerel 189
1934 stand construction 188-189
1936 brine bath 135
1936 new stand construction 56
1937 supporters 307
1954 flood 291
1961 Cheshunt training ground 340-341
1961 double-winning team 340-341
1962 FA Cup Final 200-201
1962 v. Glasgow Rangers, ticket rush 268-269
Beal, Phil 370
Chivers, Martin 370
Greaves, Jimmy 42-43, 110, 348-349
Grimsdell, Arthur 136
Tower of London guards in snow 354-355
Trafalgar Square
1933 Everton supporter FA Cup Final 360
1933 Manchester City supporters FA Cup Final 361
1949 Scotland supporters 303
1963 FA Cup Final ticket protest 108
training
1932 Chelsea 64
1938 Wolverhampton Wanderers automated crossing mach

1950 Arsenal ball-propelling machine 156
1957 Wrexham 65
1962 Arsenal 96-97
1963 Chelsea tactics 240
1965 Birmingham City shooting skills 157
1966 Chelsea goalkeepers 146-147
Tranmere Rovers, Dave Russell 204-205
treatment
brine bath 135
shower massage 76
ice bath 166
sunlamp 346-347
turkish bath 167
turkish bath 167

U
Upton Park see West Ham United

V
Valley, The see Charlton Athletic
Vaughan, Frankie 68
Venables, Terry 180-181, 260-261, 292-293, 370-371
village game 14-15
'Vogue' photograph 344-345

W
Wadell, Willie 250
Wales v. England deaf and dumb teams 1925: 161
Wales, HRH Prince of 60
walking noticeboard 320
Walsall, Ernest Wilson 86
Walsh, Billy 247
Walthamstow Schoolboys 98
Warren, Ray 290
Warwick, A 362
Watford
Cotterill, Frank 350-351
Higgins, Bert 280-281
McLaren, Jim 19
weather see flares, floods, frost, ice, snow
weatherbeaters 151
Webb, Dave 370, 370-371
Webbers 29
Welsh, Don 219
Wembley Stadium
1923 construction 132-133
1923 flagpole 132
1930 FA Cup Final from the air 34-35
1930 Graf Zeppelin 34-35
1936 crowd control FA Cup Final 68-69
1945 box office staff 109
1953 England v. Hungary supporters 365
1964 Bobby Moore 54
1966 World Cup seat assembly 79
1968 European Cup Final 328-329
1973 community singing 68
and see FA Cup Finals
West Bromwich Albion
1931 FA Cup Final 372-373
1935 supporter 50-51
1954 FA Cup Final 378-379
Allen, Ronnie 378-379
Sanders, Jim 378-379
West Ham United
1923 supporters FA Cup Final 66-67

1930 spectators 182-183
1933 supporters 88-89
1964 FA Cup on Underground 236-237
1965 heat-treatment 12-13
1968 Reverend supporter 292-293
Burkett, Jack 12-13
Hurst, Geoff 42-43, 370-371
Johnston, Gordon 286-287
Mitchell, Warren as Alf Garnett 92
Moore, Bobby 42-43
White Hart Lane see Tottenham Hotspur
Whitehorn, Stan 204-205
Whittaker, Tom 362
Wilson, Alec 156
Wilson, Ernest 86
Wilson, Joe 76
Wilson, Ray 42-43
Wilson, Yates 362
Wisdom, Norman 172
Wiseman, D. 118-119
Wolverhampton Wanderers
1938 automated crossing machine 18
1939 malted milk 33
1949 supporter 93
1949 supporters 211
1950 FA Cup 3rd round tie 220-221
1952 turkish bath 167
Flowers, Ron 42-43
Sims, Nigel 167
'Woman's Realm' photograph 345
World Cup 1936
Ashington parade 366
ball selection 28
Charlton, Bobby 366
Charlton, Jack 366
Charlton, Mrs Cissie 248-249
England squad on day before Final 352-353
England v. Argentina 130-131
engraved crystal ball 324
Jules Rimet trophy 264-265
Pickles (dog) 264-265
police duty 359
Ramsey, Alf 324
Wembley stadium seat assembly 79
World War I 1914-1918 178
World War II 1939-1945
Arsenal team in military uniforms 218
disabled ex-servicemen 179
spectators at Stamford Bridge 52-53
three Army sergeants 219
Wrexham 1957 training 65
Wright, Bill 104-105
Wright, Billy 238, 239
Wright, Tom 38-39

Y
'Ye Silent Twins' supporters 252
Yeovil Town 1949 supporters 23

PHOTOGRAPHIC CREDITS
Zelda Cheatle Gallery: 330, 331
Daily Express: 106-107, 172, 209, 227, 232-233, 314, 344, 366, 378-379
Hulton Getty: endpapers, jacket front, 9, 10-11, 12-13, 16-17, 18, 19, 20-21, 24-25, 26-27, 28, 30-31, 33, 34, 36-37, 40, 40-41, 42-43, 48-49, 50-51, 51, 52-53, 54, 55, 56, 56-57, 60, 60-61, 62-63, 64, 66-67, 68, 72-73, 73, 74, 75, 77, 80-81, 88-89, 90, 90-91, 92, 93, 94-95, 98, 99, 100-101, 102, 110, 113, 114-115, 115, 116, 117, 118, 118-119, 120-121, 121, 122-123, 126-127, 128, 130-131, 132, 132-133, 134-135, 135, 136, 137, 138, 140, 142-143, 147, 148-149, 154-155, 157, 158-159, 160-161, 161, 163, 166, 167, 168-169, 170, 170-171, 174-175, 176-177, 178, 179, 180-181, 182-183, 188-189, 189, 190-191, 192-193, 194-195, 196, 199, 200, 202-203, 206-207, 208-209, 210, 211, 214, 215, 218, 222, 224-225, 228-229, 230, 240, 242-243, 246, 247, 248-249, 252-253, 253, 256-257, 258, 259, 260-261, 261, 262, 263, 264-265, 266-267, 270, 271, 272, 273, 274, 275, 276-277, 278-279, 280-281, 285, 288-289, 290, 291, 292-293, 294, 296-297, 302-303, 304, 305, 306, 307, 310, 312, 313, 316, 317, 318-319, 320, 321, 322-323, 324, 326-327, 332-333, 333, 334, 336-337, 337, 342, 343, 346-347, 347, 350, 350-351, 352-353, 354-355, 358, 359, 360, 361, 364, 366-367, 368-369, 374-375
Littlewoods Pools: 44, 45
Popperfoto: jacket back, 14-15, 24, 29, 32, 38-39, 46-47, 65, 68-69, 71, 82-83, 84, 85, 86, 96-97, 103, 104-105, 105, 108, 109, 110-111, 159, 164-165, 173, 186, 187, 196-197, 219, 223, 226, 231, 238, 239, 244-245, 245, 265, 282, 283, 286-287, 295, 298-299, 300-301, 303, 310-311, 323, 328-329, 338, 340-341, 362, 362-363, 372-373, 376, 377
Private collection: 356-357
Science & Society Picture Library: 22, 70, 76, 78, 79, 112, 140-141, 144-145, 150, 184, 184-185, 198, 216-217, 220-221, 241, 250, 251, 254-255, 268-269, 308-309, 325, 334-335, 339, 365, 374
Terry O'Neill: 212-213, 370, 371
Topham Picturepoint: 23, 34-35, 58, 59, 86-87, 124-125, 129, 139, 142, 146-147, 151, 152-153, 156, 162-163, 200-201, 204-205, 234-235, 236-237, 249, 284-285, 314-315, 345, 348-349

Cassell & Co acknowledge the assistance provided by Charles Merullo and colleagues in the Publishing Projects Department at Getty Images/Hulton Getty.

Hulton|Archive

ACKNOWLEDGEMENTS

For Julie,
United Forever...

My special thanks are due to
Steve Guise, Colin Jacobson and Jack Tennant who
contributed enormously to this project.

My thanks also to old and new friends for their patience, support and expertise:

Alan Ashby, Marcel Ashby, Neil Burgess, Gordon Burn,
Patrick Carpenter, Zelda Cheatle, Sue Cranmer, Clive Crook,
Nick Culpeper, Mark Debnam, Stuart Dempster, Tony Eyles,
Terry Fincher, Mike Freeman, Nick Goater, David Godwin,
Paul Goodman, Carol Gorner, Brendan and Deborah Hayes,
Suzanne Hodgart, Justin Hunt, Penny Jones, Shem Law,
Margaret Little, Rodney Marsh, Roger Mayne, Caroline Metcalfe,
John Mitchinson, Chris Myers, Amanda Nevill, Terry O'Neill,
Michael Rand, David Robson, Don Stick, Alice Tennant,
Jamie Trendall, Louise Walker, Adam Ward, Jon Waters.
And my Mum and Dad, of course, for that 1963 Cup Final ticket...

Picture sources:

Phil Burnham-Richards, Joelle Ferly, Charles Merullo and Liz Ihre at Hulton Getty,
Brian Liddy and Anne Bucktrout at the National Museum of Photography, Film & Television,
Angela Murphy and Venita Paul at Science & Society Picture Library,
Liz Pendleton at Littlewoods Pools,
Alan Smith and Mark Dowd at Topham Picturepoint,
Andrew Wrighting, Sylvia Duffin and David Upton at Popperfoto.

All Football clubs and organisations who helped with caption detail, particularly:

David Barber at the Football Association, Ian Cook at Arsenal,
Peter Hall at Plymouth Argyle, Graham Hughes at Wolverhampton Wanderers,
Phil Noble at Manchester City, Andy Porter and John Rayner at Tottenham Hotspur,
Peter Stewart at West Ham, Richard Walker at Watford, Ted Wilding at Millwall.

... and Bruce Bernard.